DATE DUE

THE WORLD
AND
RIDGEWAY,
SOUTH CAROLINA

by Urban Whitaker and Bruce E. Davis

Studies In International Affairs No. 5

INSTITUTE OF INTERNATIONAL STUDIES

UNIVERSITY OF SOUTH CAROLINA

Columbia   1967

Manufactured in the United States of America

TO THE MEMORY OF

CHARLES O. LERCHE

Son of the North
Student of the South
Friend of all peoples

FOREWORD

In recent years scholarship in International Relations has turned increasingly to the study of political development and modernization. Thousands of American field researchers have descended upon the newly emerged states of the world to study at firsthand the impact of modern communications, commerce, and industry on the processes of politics and nation building. The scholars have increasingly found that the analytical tools, the research methods, and particularly the terminology of only a generation ago are inadequate. With justification they have lamented the inapplicability of the clichés and stereotypes associated with surveys of static political structures and have called for accent on the dynamics of change, development, and differentiation in the study of the many new actors on the stage of world politics.

It is, however, an interesting commentary on the state of international relations research, perhaps on our ethnocentrism, that many of the developments which have excited the energies of researchers abroad, and which they insist must have close scrutiny before the foreign policies of the new states can be understood, have gone unexamined in the United States. In the country where mass communications, particularly television, are having probably the most extensive and profound impact on education, journalism, politics, and culture, the clichés and stereotypes of former analyses are even more outmoded. It is too frequently forgotten that the United States is probably the most rapidly developing country in the world. Because we often categorize ourselves as a "developed country", we forget to apply to the study of the United States and its world relations the very methods which are uncovering data about political development in societies abroad.

This volume, the fifth in the series of Studies in International Affairs, published by the Institute of International Studies, confirms the need for attention to aspects of political development in the United States. Professor Urban Whitaker of San Francisco State College was a visiting professor at the University of South Carolina during the academic year 1965-1966. During that period, he and Mr. Bruce Davis, a graduate student in the Department of International Studies, conducted the field research on which this book reports. Their study has wide-ranging implications and importance, not the least of which is the need for further work along these lines.

Though at first glance one would hardly suppose that a report on political attitudes in a small South Carolina town of less than four hundred people would be significant, it is. Whitaker and Davis make clear the extent to which the American South is becoming nationalized; they demonstrate the importance of television and other mass media in attitude formation; and they show the manner in which citizens in a small American community relate to problems of international relations. But most important, their research has indicated the need for attention to dynamics and change in the various geographical regions of the United States. Images, generalizations, static interpretations, and stereotypes about various regions are as outmoded for purposes of analysis of America's world role as they are for our current studies of the "developing areas," areas which are likely not developing as rapidly as the United States.

The authors urge more planned exchange of scholars and students between the South and other areas. Perhaps it would not be far off the mark to suggest the need for more systematic educational exchange among all the regions of this large and diverse country. Surely this volume offers one concrete example of the value which could accrue from such a program.

RICHARD L. WALKER,
*James F. Byrnes Professor of
International Relations.*

Columbia, South Carolina,
July 21, 1967.

CONTENTS

CONTENTS–Continued

PREFACE

"It is generally accepted among thoughtful people that in a democracy like ours an informed public opinion is an essential condition of effective U. S. foreign policy performance." These are the opening words of Max F. Millikan, president of the World Peace Foundation, in his foreword to Alfred O. Hero's book *Americans in World Affairs*. The foreword goes on to point out that too little is known about the ways in which public opinion is formed. Writing in 1959, Mr. Millikan noted that "the fund of research findings focused directly on these questions [about the formation of world affairs attitudes] is rather scanty."[1]

To improve our understanding in this field of study, the World Peace Foundation has directly sponsored a number of projects. Mr. Hero's 1959 book summarizes the research which had been done to that date and suggests many subjects for further study. One of these is the detailed study of various geographical-cultural regions of the United States. In 1965 Hero himself published *The Southerner and World Affairs*, which traces the trends in Southern opinion, studies different Southern interest groups, and discusses probable future developments.[2] A companion volume that grew out of the same research and focuses particularly on the voting patterns of Southern Congressmen was published by our late colleague Charles O. Lerche, Jr., in 1964.[3]

---

[1] Quoted in Alfred O. Hero, *Americans in World Affairs* (World Peace Foundation, 1959), pp. i, ii.
[2] Hero, *The Southerner and World Affairs* (Baton Rouge: Louisiana State University Press, 1965).
[3] Charles O. Lerche, *The Uncertain South: Its Changing Patterns of Politics in Foreign Policy* (Chicago: Quadrangle Press, 1964).

The Ridgeway project described in this book has no formal connection with these undertakings of the World Peace Foundation, but it has been influenced, encouraged, and guided by the findings recorded in the pioneering efforts of Hero and Lerche. This present research was also undertaken for the purpose of further developing our understanding of the ways in which public opinion is formulated and expressed. There are two primary differences between the Ridgeway project and most of the other work that has been done in this general field of study. First, this project was an intensive study of a very small area, the town of Ridgeway, South Carolina, one mile long, one-half mile wide, and the home of 397 Americans in a rural county of the Deep South. Second, this project was directed primarily toward the study of attitudes about just one element in world affairs, the United Nations.

As an intensive study of attitudes on one major subject our work not only stands in marked contrast to the Hero and Lerche publications, which covered the whole Southern region and studied a wide spectrum of attitudes, but extends and complements them. Throughout the text we have measured our findings in the small town of Ridgeway against those of other researchers who have studied the South as a whole. While these comparisons cannot lead to conclusive results (our study was later by several years than most of the others with which we have compared, and our methods were quite different), we believe that there are some significant variations in our findings which may point the way toward further areas of productive research on the long-neglected local levels.

Our conclusions are summarized in the introductory chapter and described in detail in chapters III and IV. Implicit in our conclusions are several recommendations for further study. We are particularly hopeful that other students of the South (from anywhere in the land) will take advantage of the exceptional research opportunities which this area offers in the broad field of international studies.

We have described our methods at considerable length in chapter V and have commented in chapters VI and VII on the reliability and applicability of our findings. Our approach was unique and, we believe, opened many avenues of study and understanding not available through more conventional studies. We are a professor and a graduate student. Urban Whitaker is professor of international relations at San Francisco State College and was on leave for the 1965–'6 academic year, when he was visiting professor in the Department of International Studies, University of South Carolina. Bruce Davis, a native of Lancaster, South Carolina, and a graduate of Furman University, was a graduate student in the Department of International Studies for the same academic year.

For a period of nine months (September 1965 through May 1966) we visited regularly in Ridgeway and the surrounding areas of Fairfield County. Our primary research method was the personal interview in an informal setting. During the nine months of study we talked with nearly 80 per cent of those who live or work in the town of Ridgeway and with many others who live nearby or have some interest in or knowledge of the town. For other researchers or interested students we have described our methods in some detail in chapter VI, and we have appended copies of our interviewing schedules and other pertinent data.

A complete list of all those who assisted us in this project would fill many pages. At the University of South Carolina we are particularly indebted to Professor Raymond A. Moore, Jr., to our other colleagues in the Department of International Studies, to Professor John McConaughy, and to Mary Mansfield and Cloris DeGroot. At San Francisco State College we were ably assisted by Joseph R. Harbert both in the collection of data and in the preparation of the population table in Appendix III. In Ridgeway we are particularly grateful to Mayor Robert Thomas, Mrs. Nancy Ruff, Mr. Mood Harrison, and Mr. T. Cook, who gave us many extra hours of help. We cannot, however, adequately express our appreciation to many, many others in Ridgeway and Winnsboro who were always willing to go out of their way to help us.

Finally, we appreciate the advice and criticism of many colleagues around the country. Our work was especially inspired and assisted by Alfred O. Hero, of the World Peace Foundation, and Dean Charles Lerche, of American University, to whom this book is dedicated.

Because they suffered all the usual inconveniences of authors' wives and also because they collaborated in the development of our thinking as close and able critics, we record our appreciation to Jean Whitaker and Rachel Davis.

URBAN WHITAKER
San Francisco, California

BRUCE DAVIS
Macon, Georgia

February 27, 1967

I

INTRODUCTION

We are shocked. As the shock sets in more deeply, we realize that we have suffered not one but two shattering experiences. First, we are—perhaps excusably—shocked to find that attitudes toward the United Nations in the small, Deep Southern town of Ridgeway, South Carolina, are not much different from those found in Berkeley, California. Second, we are shocked at ourselves and at the vast majority of our fellow citizens who think as we used to think about small towns of the Deep South.

We set out in September 1965 expecting to find some factual evidence to prove what everybody "knows"—that fear and hatred of the United Nations is one of many very bad characteristics of most small towns of the Deep South. Instead, we proved that this common belief is wrong. We believe that what we found out about attitudes toward the United Nations in Ridgeway has significance far beyond the rather narrow bounds of our specific study. While we cannot offer firm evidence that Ridgeway is typical of every rural area in the Deep South, our research strongly suggests the following conclusions: (1) the South in general, and the rural Deep South in particular, is rapidly becoming nationalized; (2) there is a dramatically large lag in Northern and Western understanding of the South, and vice versa; (3) a major program of accelerated cultural exchange inside the United States ought to receive priority attention.

We want to discuss each of these points at some length before our more specific report about attitudes toward the United Nations in Ridgeway. In many ways these tentative conclusions are merely by-products of our work. We were not studying the processes of nationalization. Indeed, we assumed that they had not advanced very far. Nor did we intend to become concerned about Northern and Southern images of each other. And we did not intend that our year's study should result in any recommendations. In a very real sense we were shocked into these. We report them and comment upon them not so much because we have studied them as because they have persistently penetrated the studies we have done. We offer these observations not as conclusions but rather as points of departure for further studies which we believe are urgently needed.

The Nationalization of the South

So far as our specific area of research is concerned, we report with confidence (chapter IV below) that there are only minor differences between the South and the rest of the country. After interviewing nearly 80 per cent of the adults in Ridgeway (population: 397), we found only one person who considered himself "strongly opposed" to the United Nations and only 4 per cent who expressed "opposition" rather than "no opinion" (33 per cent) or "favorable" (over 62 per cent).

These results, of course, do not conclusively prove that the South is being nationalized, even in terms of its attitudes toward the United Nations. Perhaps it has always been so. Perhaps on this particular subject there have never been serious regional differences. But there is much evidence to the contrary in the works of other writers. Our own work has led us into other areas and left us with so many by-products that we are emboldened at least to offer these brief comments about a broad, across-the-board process of nationalization which is reconstructing the South.

We do not pretend to be experts or even full-time students of economics or sociology or of such specific problem areas as communications, transportation, or race relations. Yet we have been able to observe at close range the forces of economic and social change at work in Southern communities. We offer our brief remarks on these subjects in the form of comments on a thesis which is gaining widespread acceptance in the South: that the South is America's new frontier and that very rapidly it will catch and eventually surpass the rest of the country.

If we assume certain values (arguments in support of which we do not undertake to set forth here), the South can prove this thesis only if it accomplishes at least the following aspects of what amounts to a vital economic and social transformation: more industrialization; a much higher rate of productive employment: expanded opportunities for a good education; and firm guarantees, *de facto* as well as *de jure*, of political and social freedom, i.e., the elimination of discrimination based on race.

While these are vitally interrelated developments, we are convinced that they all depend finally on progress in the elimination of social discrimination. The economy will boom healthily and permanently only if all the population is well enough educated to hold the kinds of jobs which are characteristic of the advancing technological age and to earn the kind of money which makes them good customers. In short, economic progress requires educational progress if either production or consumption can be maintained at high levels.

The educational prerequisities in turn depend on the elimination of segregationist practices which in the past have held in place a vicious circle of inferior education offered to Negroes by other Negroes who got inferior education from still other Negroes whose training was inferior. Paradoxically one of the apparent attractions the South offers to industry is cheap labor and other low costs. In fact, where costs are low because educational standards are low, the opportunities for profit making are also restricted by the low buying power of poorly educated potential customers.

While recognizing that many other factors are relevant, we believe that the ultimate test of the South's ability to catch and surpass the rest of the country must be met in the area of race relations. Indeed, this is specifically what many Southerners have in mind when they say they will soon move out ahead of their Northern and Western compatriots.

The argument runs like this: the purely legal phase of the civil rights movement will soon have run its course all over the country. When Negroes have the full franchise and the full rights to public accommodations, including educational facilities, any regional differences in Negro rights will depend on the abilities of the races to live together in fact. The contention—and we do not want to give the impression that we believe it is shared by all Southerners— is that the South is better prepared for this eventuality that is the inexperienced North.

We believe that there is much to support this conclusion. Lily-white communities and black ghettos literally blanket the non-

Southern areas of the United States. Race riots are much more often reported from Chicago, Detroit, Los Angeles, and New York than from Atlanta, Charleston, Birmingham, and New Orleans.

On the other hand, it may be that riots in the ghettos of the North and West take place in conditions which the South has simply not yet reached rather than to which it is immune. If Watts was bad, what are we to expect in an industrialized but still ghettoized Columbia, South Carolina, in the 1980s or 1990s?

The defense of the thesis that the South has peculiar advantages rests partly on the assertion that Southern whites are better acquainted with Negroes than are their Northern and Western neighbors. It all boils down to the thought that in spite of all the full-scale *de jure* segregation in the South's past, there is significant advantage to the South's future in the *de facto* integration that has always been a characteristic of Southern society. Children have played together regardless of color. Whites are quite used to having Negroes in their homes, so long as the differential economic and social status remains quite clear. One can hardly imagine more intimate experiences between two human beings than the suckling of the young, which was not always strictly segregated in the Old South. Much more widespread in the experience of contemporary Southerners are domestic associations with Negro maids, cooks, handymen, etc. It remains to be seen whether these associations—physical intimacies in an atmosphere of social inequality—will prove to be better preparation for the future than will a common Northern and Western pattern of virtual physical isolation in an atmosphere of legal but often meaningless equality.

Clearly Southerners as a group have more experience at interracial association than have other Americans. Interracial friendships in the South are both much more numerous and much deeper than outsiders generally believe. Such factors may make a difference in the South's ability to adapt once the legal barriers are down. Even in housing the South may have some advantage of experience. Negroes and whites have been next-door neighbors (often, it is true, with the one in a shack and the other in a mansion) for many decades. See the nearly—but not exclusively—segregated housing pattern in Ridgeway, for example, as shown by the map in appendix IV.

Another element that may contribute to the South's ability to catch or surpass the rest of the country in race relations is the phenomenon of "take-off." Many Southern forces for moderation and change which have been immobilized by a feeling of hopelessness for many years are being freed by the winds of change. As they begin to express themselves, there may appear to be dramatic changes of opinion in areas where, in fact, relatively small changes in the prevailing balance have simply given public vent to liberal feeling long held in silence. This take-off phenomenon may be especially marked among businessmen and politicians who, after all, have natural inclinations to satisfy customers and voting constituents.

We reiterate the fact that we claim no particular expertise on these subjects. Nor did we set out to study the proposition that across-the-board nationalization is an emerging pattern in the Deep South. But our studies have led us unavoidably into this related field. At the very least, we believe that the nationalization thesis deserves widespread study and discussion. We have found that television in particular, and the communication-transportation revolution in general, are very rapidly nationalizing Ridgeway's attitudes toward the United Nations. We strongly suspect that it is true of other communities and on other subjects. In fact, we see no reason to believe that these processes stop at national borders. Perhaps what is happening in the South today is only a preview of what will occur throughout the world tomorrow.

Cultural Lag in the North

We do not mean by the title of these paragraphs to discriminate against the Northern and Western parts of the United States which surround the Deep South. What we have to say about failures of understanding are true for all regions. But somehow it is more shocking (at least for non-Southerners) to discover the depth of misunderstanding about the South that exists in otherwise well-informed circles of outsiders. The problem is the worse for the fact that it is often a very active misunderstanding, i.e., it infects those who firmly hold, and regularly act upon, strong ideas about the tenor of Southern life. We are aware, for example, of numerous instances in which well-educated college professors have declined offers to teach in the South because they were afraid—afraid that they could not speak their minds freely, afraid that their children could not find decent schools, afraid in some instances for their physical well-being. We know that there is a great distance between Northern images and Southern realities. The South has some unique problems, but they are regularly and very badly overdrawn.

The patterns of misconception run both ways. For example, the authors are acquainted with a young man in the South who wanted to accept an invitation to visit San Francisco but did not because he was afraid of violence. His impression rested primarily on newspaper stories about the Watts Riots (actually in the Los Angeles area, four hundred miles from San Francisco) and the "Hell's Angels," a marauding band of motorcyclists. To San Franciscans the notion is absurd (although that city has since had riots severe enough to require a curfew in certain residential areas.) But in the vast majority of Southern communities it is absurd to imagine that outsiders would be afraid to live in, visit, or even to pass through the Deep South.

The point is that both the North and the South are very big and very diverse places. There are many liberals in the South and quite a few active racist reactionaries outside the South. No region of the United States is characterized by violence. Major news stories often do, but never should, lead us to vivid generalizations about whole regions which are not even accurate for small cities. The reporter who wrote that "violence is the order of the day" for the small Southern town was simply wrong. Racial violence is rare almost everywhere in the United States almost all the time.

Risking the usual dangers of oversimplification, we would argue that the whole of the United States suffers, in the mid 1960's, from what might be described as a "Berkeley-Bogalusa" complex. A little news from either place goes much too far toward making too many people much too sure that "California is like that" or that "It's just what one would expect in the South."

Again, we emphasize that although we have lived and traveled extensively in the South, we have studied in detail only one small town and specifically only its attitudes toward the United Nations. But our study has called into serious question a number of generalizations which we believe to be widely held all over the United States. (See in particular Table E, which records the expectations of both California and South Carolina college students about U.N. attitudes in Ridgeway.)

An Intra-American Cultural Exchange Program

All regions of the United States are already benefiting to some degree from a cultural intermingling that has grown rapidly in recent years. We believe, however, that the time has come for a planned program of exchanges between the South and other areas. We do not comment here on such visitors to the South as the civil rights workers, whose mission is primarily to change conditions. Rather we have in mind a program of year-long "live in" exchanges of students, teachers, and others who come more to learn about their neighbors than to teach them new ways. We are convinced that no area of the United States is immune to the advantages that accrue from such arrangements.

The Relevance of Ridgeway

Perhaps our studies in Ridgeway are not so relevant as to justify such sweeping conclusions. Yet we have found that the story told in the following pages is as surprising to others— both within and outside the South—as it was to us.

We have tried to find out how the 397 people of this small South Carolina town obtain their information about world affairs, what they think of the United Nations, and what they do to give effect to their attitudes. We are frank to admit that we began with the idea (held more firmly by the visiting Californian than by the native South Carolinian) that Ridgeway would be well out of the mainstream of American thought. Specifically we expected to find that both races would consider the U.N. primarily in terms of civil rights and that the Whites would be, therefore, generally opposed to the world organization. What we found instead is described in the remainder of this book.

II

AN INTRODUCTION TO RIDGEWAY

The Town and Its People

Ridgeway is a particularly appropriate name for this settlement of 397 people. The town takes its name from the ridge that bisects the lower area of Fairfield County between the Broad and the Wateree rivers. When the Charlotte and South Carolina Railroad, of which Mr. Edward G. Palmer, of Ridgeway, was the first president, was completed in 1850, the new railroad followed the ridge north of Columbia toward Winnsboro. Ridgeway, at an elevation of 625 feet above sea level, is the highest point on the Southern Railway between Augusta, Georgia, and Charlotte, North Carolina. This high elevation tends to cause weather reports out of Charlotte (72 miles north) to be a more reliable prediction of Ridgeway's weather than weather reports out of Columbia (24 miles south).

The town limits, measuring exactly one mile in length and one-half mile in width, and the immediately surrounding countryside are the site of several beautiful antebellum houses.

The most imposing building in the town of Ridgeway is the Century House. Using lumber and material procured mostly from the plantation and bricks made by slave labor, the massive, two-story, solid brick house, located almost in the center of town and shaded by large and ancient trees, was completed in 1854 by James Buchanan Coleman, an extensive landowner.

The Brick House has entertained many visitors. But its most distinguished occupant was General P. G. T. Beauregard, commanding general of the Confederate forces of the Deep South, who, having evacuated Columbia with the approach of General Sherman's northward advancing Union Army, chose Ridgeway as Confederate headquarters both because of its railroad and telegraph office and because of its strategic location in relationship to Columbia, Camden, Charleston, and Wilmington. Coleman's Brick House was used for General Beauregard and his staff's accommodation February 17–19, 1865. "These three days and the three following remain the busiest and most exciting week in the history of Ridgeway and Fairfield." [1]

Today the Century House serves as the social center of the community. It is headquarters for entertainments of all kinds, some of which the authors had the good fortune to attend. The big building also houses the Ridgeway branch of the Fairfield County Library.

Several outstanding examples of old Southern plantation houses grace Ridgeway's immediately surrounding countryside. The one with the richest historical heritage is called Valencia. Built in 1834 by Edward Gendron Palmer, it rests upon a high, verdant hill overlooking lush, green woodlands as far as the eye can see. It was first called Bloomingdale. The name, however, was changed upon the suggestion of Mrs. Palmer's brother, James Davis II, who had just returned from a grand tour of Europe during which he had spent much time in Spain. So much did the view from his sister's home remind Mr. Davis of the landscape seen from his hotel room in Valencia that he suggested they rename the new manor house for that Spanish city.

The large two-story frame house with a broad piazza across the front is reminiscent of the plantation houses found in the Low Country. The long, spacious halls and large, high-ceilinged, elegantly decorated rooms are filled with priceless heirlooms and rare documents. The past is so well remembered at Valencia that the home is like a museum of Southern history. Among the most cherished of these things of times past are a small table that once belonged to Thomas Jefferson and a lock of hair taken from the head of South Carolina's celebrated son and one of the United States Senate's most famous members, John C. Calhoun. But what is perhaps Valencia's most prized possession is a document signed by Mr. Palmer swearing allegiance to the Union and to President Andrew Johnson. The plantation owner was most reluctant to sign this special "oath of Allegiance" after the civil conflict and died a

---

[1] Julian Bolick, *A Fairfield Sketchbook* (Winnsboro, S. C.: Jacobs Brothers, 1963), p. 28.

short time after so doing. The document is now framed and hangs on a wall in the drawing room at Valencia.

The plantation and house still belong to the Palmer family. The age of the old frame house causes its occupants so much concern about its safety from fire that it is never left unattended for more than very short periods.

These and other lovely and interesting antebellum houses in the county which contained South Carolina's two largest slaveholding families tell of a fading past when "cotton was king" in Ridgeway, as it was in most of the South. But large-scale cotton agriculture has been dead for some time in Fairfield County, and what little cotton is still planted here is a practice born more of nostalgia than of economic incentive. Ridgeway, along with the rest of the South, is making the move to an industrially oriented economy. For example, one man who once planted almost all of his extensive landholding in cotton has cut his annual planting to only twenty acres. Most of his land now lies fallow or is planted in soil conservation crops. His once-busy cotton gin, located in Ridgeway, is falling into a state of disrepair.

A second very telling indication of the economic change taking place in Ridgeway is the conversion of once-numerous cotton fields into green acres of pine forest. Remembering how it once was. Ridgeway's best-known senior citizen recalls that "those were the days when cotton was king and I loved it. Nowadays I go riding out in the country and see all those pine trees and I think, 'Oh, wouldn't that be nice in cotton.'" But attesting most strongly to the change in Ridgeway's economic base is the fact that no in-town Negroes make their living as independent farmers or sharecroppers, and only two in-town Whites earn their living as tillers of the soil. Interestingly enough, these two are not poor Whites. There are, so far as we can tell, only two families of poor Whites within the town limits of Ridgeway. Not having interviewed many such families, we cannot say either where they went or what they think. It is our guess that their conspicuous absence in Ridgeway is largely attributable to a move from Ridgeway to points closer to their jobs —a move made necessary by the costs of daily commuting from Ridgeway to Winnsboro, Great Falls, or Columbia. Ridgeway's Negro families, almost all of whom are an appallingly long way from affluence, have a number of primary breadwinners who have employment outside of Ridgeway. Commuting cost is for them a particularly burdensome expense. However, many of Ridgeway's families, both Negro and White, have no choice but to bear it because Ridgeway's one major source of employment is the pulpwood mill which hires only a few of the town's unskilled laborers. Other workers, not owning or employed by in-town businesses, commute to jobs in Columbia, to the U. S. Rubber Company and the Manhattan Shirt Company in Winnsboro (11 miles west), or to the J. P. Stevens textile mill in Great Falls (13 miles north). A few others, mostly skilled workers, find employment at the Fairview nursing home and alcoholic rehabilitation center located four miles east of Ridgeway. Six of Ridgeway's White women are employed as teachers at the integrated Ridgeway elementary school. The Geiger (Negro) elementary school faculty is comprised entirely of out-of-town personnel, mostly from Columbia.

At least two thirds of Ridgeway's in-town White working group qualify as skilled workmen, i.e., professional personnel (10), government employees (3), white collar workers (15), public school teachers (6), managerial personnel (3), businessmen (10), other skilled workmen, e.g., electricians and carpenters, (11), and four policemen. Sixteen of Ridgeway's citizens enjoy the leisure of fulltime retirement and four are unemployed. Only three of Ridgeway's in-town Negroes qualify as skilled workmen; three others are unemployed and six are retired. The others work at unskilled jobs.[2]

A Ridgeway redevelopment organization was created for the purpose of bringing good-paying industrial jobs within the people's local reach. However, progress toward that goal has been very slow. There is no widespread active displeasure with the organization, although most of the people are aware of the great boost local industry would provide to the town's economy. But there are some who complained to us that the few belonging to the town's landed aristocracy, not wishing to see the town's character substantially changed, have, through their absolute refusal to sell land or unwillingness to sell it for less than exorbitant prices, built an industrial by-pass around Ridgeway.[3] As one well-informed observer of the situation put it, "Industry doesn't come because the clique doesn't want it." Another of our respondents, who is also a member of the redevelopment organization, noted DuPont's, as

---

[2] While most respondents were willing to give us some information about the amount of their annual income, we were not able to calculate any accurate and meaningful figures for the town as a whole or for racial groups.

[3] In early 1967 there are strong indications that a substantial industrial enterprise will be established in Ridgeway.

well as U. S. Rubber's, wish to locate in Ridgeway. "But too much was asked for the land or the owners were unwilling to sell." Both DuPont and U. S. Rubber eventually located in South Carolina, the former in Camden and the latter in Winnsboro. Western Auto also investigated the possibilities of locating in Ridgeway but could not do so because the establishment of a new operation required a minimum of three thousand registered vehicles in the area, and Ridgeway, even counting its "suburbs," has only 990.

During the period of our interviewing there was a great deal of excited talk about the strong possibilities of a company manufacturing various kinds of piping coming to Ridgeway. This company, which would have provided approximately 75 moderately compensated unskilled jobs, did not come primarily because of its inability to negotiate a necessary purchase of land adjacent to the railroad. The virtual certainty that these jobs would have been manned by Negroes was noted by some as a reason for not becoming inordinately troubled over the loss of the 75 jobs.

Race and Religion in Ridgeway

Ridgeway's thinking about the Negro movement to achieve unqualified enjoyment of the rights of American citizenship is not as unyieldingly negative as one might expect in this small rural Deep South town. No Negro is likely to be welcomed any time soon to a community social function at the Century House because the Negro's right to attend such social functions is not yet recognized and/or admitted by enough Whites. But it is becoming generally recognized in Ridgeway that the "Negro's place" is considerably less restricted than once imagined. This progressively developing attitude is vividly reflected in remarks such as the following: "It's O.K. to be in school or church together, but not in my house or at my table." [4] "Integration is O.K. in Ridgeway. We've had no trouble and it's good for business." "I don't want integration but I can live with it." "I'm opposed to integration but I accept it because it is the law of the land." "I don't support all that's being done in the field of civil rights but I don't disagree enough to cause any trouble." "Civil rights is a coming thing and we must accept it. I'm certainly in favor of freedom. I favor equal treatment but not pre-

---

[4] Negroes and Whites are in school together in Ridgeway, but they are not in church together. One Ridgeway minister thinks it will be twenty years before Negroes will be welcomed into the membership of White congregations in Ridgeway.

ferential treatment. I support integrated education." A young man with a college education and a good-paying job "with a good organization with a good chance for advancement" thinks "the NAACP and CORE are demanding too much." But integrated educational facilities are not part of their excessive demands. He says, "I support integrated education but I feel that it should begin in the first grade and gradually work up. First graders are too young to have hatred in their hearts, and they can grow up together having mutual respect for one another. Fourteen or fifteen-year-olds have already formed hardened opinions—usually anti-Negro. Such opinions stem from their parent's viewpoints."

Some changes in the age-old attitudes are stimulated by contacts with Negroes who have demonstrated abilities which the White population does not usually associate with them. Several of Ridgeway's women who took the United Nations tour while visiting New York were very impressed by the fact that their learned and poised guide was "a Negro girl." They all agreed that "she was a really smart girl and an excellent guide."

Of course there are those among Ridgeway's Whites who still feel that a rigid, uncompromising separation of the races should be maintained, and some of them think themselves supported in this belief by the Bible. For example, one elderly woman believes that "the Bible says 'birds of a feather flock together,' which shows that it was not intended that they mix. I don't think I'll ever get used to it but I'm beginning to by seeing them go to school [across the street] together."

Another much younger resident of Ridgeway with a considerably more accurate knowledge of the biblical message noted that "the Bible says *love* thy neighbor—not *respect* thy neighbor. I don't love the Negroes but that's because of my Southern prejudice."

However, Ridgeway is burdened with those who have neither love nor respect for their Negro neighbor. One Negro lady, who works as a domestic for several of Ridgeway's White families, told of how one of her employers at times made it a practice to arbitrarily intervene in her purely personal affairs, demanding, under threat of firing her, that she report for a bit of nonregular work at times when she felt the welfare of her own family required that she be with them. One of the teachers in the integrated elementary school was described by the parents of a pupil in this teacher's class as an "active racist" who "preaches the racist philosophy in the classrooms and encourages the White children, through refusal to reprimand them, in displays of bigotry and racial hatred."

However, the strict segregationists are losing ground in Ridgeway. A leisurely and candid conversation with another teacher in the integrated Ridgeway elementary school who "at first bitterly opposed mixing in school" and "thought she could never accept it" revealed one of the strong reasons why this is so. This teacher has changed her mind—"just since the schools have been made to integrate"—and now finds the Negro's presence with Whites in school "acceptable." In describing her first agonizing experiences with the new situation, she said, "The first day I came I couldn't drink after them on a hot day. But why did I feel that way? I decided at home that I would drink the next day no matter how black the one who drank before me. The Negro boys using the boys' bathroom did not bother me; but the girls in the girls' room really upset me. I guess I thought their using it would have contaminated the bath facilities. It was all like taking a dose of medicine; but I now accept it as being O.K."

This teacher's first experience with integrated education has caused her to feel that "many Negroes could amount to more if given more opportunity." However, she admits this reluctantly because she "still feels there is a difference."

This lady has heard a lot and believed a lot of what she heard. She has now seen a lot and will see still more that may eventually dispel her prejudiced fears and cause her to realize that the difference is only the superficial one of skin color.

It is our feeling that the White people of Ridgeway, although unwilling actively to support, are willing to accept, changes in race relations without making an obnoxious fuss about it. It is as one of the leaders of the Negro community said: "They will do only what they are made to do and no more. If it were not for the force of the United States government, we would still be in the same category we were in three hundred years ago." The Negro's observation is reinforced by one of the town's White leaders who summed it up succinctly, "We got to accept it and we will."

Ridgeway's Negro community is comprised of the pacified, the afraid, and the fearless foresighted who work for and anxiously await the high noon of the new day they know is dawning for them.

The perfect picture of the pacified Negro is drawn by the remark of a sixty-five-year-old Negro woman who works as a maid for twelve dollars a week and a relatively nice place to stay "willed to me by my employer for as long as I lives." With undoubtable honesty this woman said, "I live happy. Whites have been good to me all my life, and I wouldn't put White folks down for all the coloreds in the world." She opposes integration and "dares anybody to come and ask me for anything." The younger Negro's persistent pressure for change is for her a mean and confusing thing. "Younger people have got such a different idea that you can't hardly realize them, or I can't."

An example of the Negro who "realizes" but has been made afraid by reports from Alabama, Mississippi, and Louisiana of how frightened Whites threaten, and on occasion actually inflict, death on those who actively seek a more equitable social arrangement is seen in the observation of a seventy-year-old Negro woman with less than a year of formal education. "Separate education is fine just so long as they get the same thing. Peace and satisfaction is better than anything you can have—it's sometimes better than money. But you see, I don't want nobody to kill my child. I want my child to live."

There are a few Negroes in Ridgeway whose preference for segregated schooling is motivated not by fear but by honest choice. They feel that as long as the Negro schools list the same course titles in their curriculum as the White schools, the Negro child in Negro schools enjoys educational opportunities equal to those of the White child in White schools. However, this is the honest opinion of far fewer Ridgeway Negroes than many Whites in Ridgeway desperately believe it to be; it is an opinion that can be found almost nowhere but among a few of the elderly for whom the time for doing and becoming has past. For many of the old and most of the young the observation by one of Ridgeway's best-educated, conscientious, and capable Negroes indicates how they stand on this matter. "There is no such monster as separate but equal," he said. "Equal opportunity requires the integration of society." A sixteen-year-old boy at Fairfield High School, who plans for a military career because "there a man can show what he can do," likes President Johnson because "he has carried out President Kennedy's program of civil rights." An elderly Negro man (seventy-one years old) likes civil rights "on one account—it lets our children go to better schools so they can get better education." Placing an arm around two of his grandchildren, he said, "These here are the ones who are going to get what they need. This here is a new day."

That it is a new day is recognized by both races in Ridgeway. And although there is no overt active hostility toward the Negro,[5] neither is there any organized biracial cooperation undertaken for the purpose of accelerating the development of this new day.

Ridgeway will not boldly and forthrightly walk into tomorrow; but neither will it have to be dragged into it kicking and screaming. It will back—reluctantly but peacefully—into tomorrow, partly because the Whites themselves are slowly changing, partly because the Negroes are not really pushing. Time nudges them both along.

One institution that might help to speed the process, the Church, has done little to challenge the status quo. The church in Ridgeway, as in most places, suffers somewhat, in the authors' opinion, from an overdose of perfunctorily performed ritual and empty formality and not enough applied Christianity. The Church's problem in Ridgeway, which is not atypical of its problem elsewhere, is to make its message relevant to the human needs and minds of our day and to inspire its people to become doers and not hearers only. "Religion," one of Ridgeway's ministers agrees, "is a matter of not what you say but of what you do."

Ridgeway has not been without a discussion from the pulpit of the question "What should one be doing about contemporary social and political problems?" During our period of interviewing (described in detail in chapter VI) in Ridgeway, a new minister and his family came to town with an alive, sensitive, and contemporary Christian faith. The realness and relevancy of this family's faith was most tellingly revealed in their relationship with their Negro neighbors. When asked how they liked working for this new minister, two Negro ladies accustomed to doing domestic chores for $3.00 a day and baby sitting services for an entire evening for $1.00, replied, "I like it because they pay me good and by the hour. For ironing I receive 75¢ an hour for flat pieces and $1.00 an hour for starched pieces." The paying of such prices for Negro maid service set off a buzz of worried concern among those paying considerably less. It was decided to communicate this concern to the minister and his wife through their children. The minister's children were urged by their friends and playmates to tell their parents that they were "paying too much for their Negro help." The urgings were silently ignored.

---

[5] There are many individual interracial friendships in Ridgeway.

Conversations with the new minister and his wife readily revealed their desire to make the Church a strong and relevant force for positive good in the community and their feeling that the first step in that direction should be the improvement of community race relations. But they were not able to imbue their parishioners with the same desire and feeling. Upon his arrival the minister was told that he was either to conform or to leave. "If you have come with any idea of changing our way of life, you might as well pack up and leave." He was "not rudely, but positively" told this. He was further instructed by his ecclesiastical superior that he was not to disturb the thinking of his parishioners. His parishioners also explicitly indicated to the minister their wish not to be bothered by sermons dealing with the major matters of consequence to the contemporary Church, such as the Church's mission today and what the Church must do if it hopes to retain or regain a meaningful hold on its members' lives.

The minister had come with an idea of changing lives, or what he would call "leading the people into an experience of new birth." But the people were not interested. Consequently the minister and his family departed for a new assignment in Pennsylvania. But before departing Ridgeway, the minister, in a sermon which the authors heard delivered, boldly burdened his people with an awareness of what they must do if they were to become truly what they profess to be. His words left no doubt that it depended on their giving and implementing an affirmative answer to the question "Am I my brother's keeper?" Conversations after the service clearly indicated that the message had stirred a useful disturbance in the thinking of those who heard.

The Church's impact on Ridgeway's thinking about world affairs will be discussed below as a part of Ridgeway's sources of information on world affairs.

Ridgeway's Politics

A study of past voting patterns and intensive interviews with Ridgeway's citizens about their choice for the presidency of the United States indicates one thing very clearly: domestic issues are far more important to them than international issues in the choice of a president. However, some of those who attach primary importance to domestic issues are not sure they should. One respondent troubled by such doubts said: "I don't know if I should give greater weight to domestic issues, because the United States is on a low ebb with other nations and nations are getting so close together its like we were all neighbors. So maybe I should give greater consideration to international issues."

The patterns of voting were not surprising. In 1960 Ridgeway (like South Carolina and the country as a whole) went to John F. Kennedy by a narrow margin over Republican Richard Nixon. In 1964 Ridgeway (mostly White voters) went for Republican nominee Barry Goldwater by about the same margin (3 to 2) as did South Carolina. In both years the Negro voters were 100 per cent for the Democratic presidential candidate. This unanimous Negro support for the Democratic candidate obviously grows out of feelings similar to those of a seventy-seven-year-old Negro man who "always liked the Democrats because I always did get a good outcome on the Democrats," and a Negro lady who likes L.B.J. because "he makes a fair way for us." A measure of the firmness of the Ridgeway Negroes' loyalty to the Democratic party can be taken from an incident recounted by one of Ridgeway's more subservient Negroes. This elderly lady told of how a White lady tried to tell her how to vote in a senatorial election. "The White lady suggested a Republican. I told the lady that nobody would tell me who to vote for. I would vote for whom I pleased, and I pleased to vote for the Democrat."

Ridgeway's Negroes receive considerable encouragement and assistance from their churches in the exercise of their newly acquired voting privileges. Negro congregations quite frequently receive political instruction from the pulpit. One minister, before each major election, has his people "write down on paper the candidate they should vote for; and all in my church vote just as I ask them." When asked why this was done, the minister explained, "It is useful —even necessary—to give such instruction in order to enlighten my people on what it all means now and will mean after awhile." Our conversation with the minister made it very clear that he looked upon the Church as providing one of the better ways of bringing mass political education to his people and information about the candidates and the one most likely to give fair treatment to Negro interests. Another of Ridgeway's Negro ministers has added an additional requirement to the Apostle Paul's list of qualifications for service as a deacon in the church. The new requirement is that deacons be registered voters. Before being ordained as a deacon, the minister "makes 'em put it [their registration certificate] on the table."

John F. Kennedy has been adopted as a virtual member of many Negro families. It is not an uncommon thing to see a large, beautifully framed and lighted portrait of the late president—who was the "first to see that Negroes need their chance"—prominently displayed in many Negro homes in Ridgeway. A young Negro man expressing his fondness for President Kennedy said, "He was like a member of the family. I just can't describe how close I felt to that man. I don't feel as close to Johnson, although I admire the marvelous way he is executing his program. If he is putting up a front, it's a good one and he's adding on good things of his own. I would vote again for L.B.J. without hesitation." President Johnson's most lofty tribute came from an elderly Negro woman on welfare who was unable to remember how few years of schooling she received. "President Johnson," she said, "is a fine man. He's putting bread in the people's mouth and doing a lot to help the people. Kennedy was all right, but I didn't get nothing when he was on. I was just fixing to get it when he passed on. But I wouldn't take nothing for Johnson. I hope he live always and never die and rest away in Jesus' arms."

Although we found many voters who said they considered both domestic and international policies in selecting a President, we found few who actually based their choice on international positions taken by candidates. In fact, "the man" and his economic policies seem to be the most vital factors. "The man," however, inevitably has something to do with race relations, and there seems little doubt that Goldwater's vote against the Civil Rights Act of 1964 won him the election in Ridgeway. With some, this was in spite of his international policies, which they considered uninformed at best and reckless at worst.

Looking to the future, Goldwater is pretty well washed up in Ridgeway. In 1966, just two years after he carried Ridgeway and South Carolina in his unsuccessful bid for the presidency, only 7 per cent chose him as the man they would most like to vote for in the 1968 presidential election. Goldwater's decline in popularity with the Ridgeway voter does not result from a disenchantment with the man or with his domestic political philosophy. The positions taken by the 1964 Republican presidential nominee are still the favorites of the majority of Ridgeway's Whites. However, the main feeling about him seems to be that "he is a loser" with little or no chance of ever being a winner. A strong supporter of Goldwater in 1964 does not favor his being renominated in 1968 because "he could not be elected." This erstwhile Goldwater supporter "would like to see

a conservative nominated who has a prospect of defeating L.B.J."
A registered Republican who voted for Goldwater "would not vote
for him again because he is too extreme and unstable and did ter-
rible damage to the Republican party." In 1966 Nixon led the Republican parade with 14.9 per cent, which gave him no better than
a tie with Johnson among White residents. Although 14.9 per cent
of the Whites indicated that they will vote for Johnson, there were
45.9 per cent who had not made any decision *except that they will
vote against L.B.J.* Opposition to the President in Ridgeway is
based primarily on the feeling that "he is spending too much
money trying to make this world a Utopia" and that he has pushed
civil rights too fast and too far. One man noted that "as Kennedy's
successor it was only natural that he push it; but we did not expect him to jam it down our throats. We thought that being a
Southerner he would understand our problems, but he obviously
does not." The President was described by almost all of his oppo-
nents in Ridgeway as a "power hungry, would-be-dictator, and a
hypocrite who has no real concern for the Negro. All he wants is
their bloc vote." There was also an appreciable amount of opposition to the President's Viet Nam policy—for example, that of a
young lady who said "L.B.J.'s Viet Nam policy is unclear. I think
he could do more to solve that conflict. I am not sure that we are
there for any good reason. But I may be bitter because my brother
is there—he's a doctor."

Ridgeway, like the rest of South Carolina and the South (as well
as other parts of the country), has a large number of nominal
Democrats who consistently vote Republican. Virtually all of them
cite the civil rights issue as their reason for voting Republican,
although the real reason may in many cases be that the Republican
party, being the more conservative party, better represents the
complete range of their political views. There are others in Ridgeway who are really Democrats on most issues except race but for
whom the race issue is reason enough not to vote for President
Johnson. Our best example of one who is a true Democrat except
on civil rights is a young man who "would like to see Truman again
as president." Our conversation with this gentleman indicated very
clearly that he preferred Truman because of his criticism of the
civil rights movement. He recalled with great delight Truman's
remark concerning the awarding of the Nobel Peace Prize to
Martin Luther King—"Well, I didn't give it to him." At the time
of this survey it appeared that Johnson will not carry Ridgeway in

1968, although he may pick up 100 per cent of the Negro vote—which is increasing—and apparently will hold onto one of every six or seven White voters. Some of Johnson's White votes in Ridgeway will come from persons like a retired elderly couple who "like L.B.J. better than expected because of his Great Society programs —especially Medicare." This couple, who voted for Nixon in 1960 and Goldwater in 1964, intend to vote for Johnson in 1968. Some more Johnson White votes will be cast by persons who remember well the Great Depression. Asked why he favored Johnson for 1968, one old gentleman replied, "Because he is a Democratic president. I'm a pretty old man and I've lived under a lot of Republican presidents and I ain't seen one yet that was not a tough proposition. You could get things cheap, but you couldn't get any money to buy them." Most of the rest of the Johnson White vote will come from those who automatically vote a Democratic ticket because "it's a family tradition."

Senator Strom Thurmond is often mentioned by Ridgeway White voters as their preference for the Presidency, one noting that he is "for Strom Thurmond for anything he runs for." But few, if any, think he has any chance. No one mentioned George Wallace. None of our interviews about the presidency gravitated naturally toward international relations.[6] And in fact, when we asked pro-Thurmond voters to comment on Thurmond's views about the United Nations, we found that they generally did not know—apparently did not vitally care—what they are. Senator Thurmond is liked in Ridgeway because he is "a man of his convictions who stands up for his own opinions whether right or wrong"; and his convictions, at least publicly and especially on civil rights, are the same as those of most of his White constituents in Ridgeway. There are a few in Ridgeway who are "no followers of Thurmond" because "he is an extremist against everything and for nothing."

The figures for Fairfield County as a whole—or for the voting area recorded as "Ridgeway" (but not the same as the town limits) —add another element to the story. Although the county voted for Kennedy by only about the same margin as did the state, four years later it went for Johnson over Goldwater by a large margin. It seems clear that there has been a substantial increase in the Negro vote. Inside the town limits the small Negro vote nearly

[6] The conduct of the survey is described in detail in chapter VI. The complete results of the survey with respect to presidential preferences are recorded in Table A of the Appendix.

doubled in 1964 (12) over 1960 (7), and new registrations through 1966 indicate that it will at least double again in 1968. Another likely factor in Fairfield's pro-Johnson vote is the fact that the county is served by a local newspaper—the Winnsboro *News and Herald*—which has consistently and unblushingly supported national Democratic party policy.

In conclusion, we find no evidence in Ridgeway to substantiate the claim that small-town Southerners are a pressure for unilateralism in foreign policy. Perhaps it can be said that they tolerate it, but they have not demanded it. Indeed, the weight of the evidence supports a contrary conclusion. If Ridgeway is like the rest of the Deep South, it is apparently correct to conclude that this region's votes in national elections are responsive primarily to domestic issues. That so many Deep South congressmen are unilateralists rather than multilateralists is probably more a by-product of conservatism on domestic issues than it is intentional on the part of the voters. By and large, the voters seem to be more progressive in international affairs than their elected representatives.

III

RIDGEWAY'S SOURCES
OF INFORMATION ON WORLD AFFAIRS

One of the worst problems which citizens in a democratic society must face is the difficulty of acquiring adequate and accurate information about world affairs. International events are so numerous and so complex that even "experts" in world politics must specialize in a limited geographical or functional area. Yet laymen are constantly called upon in the daily exercise of their duties as citizens to develop responsible attitudes on a long list of global issues. For these reasons the sources of the layman's information about world affairs becomes a vitally important part of any inquiry into attitudes.

During the course of our interviews in Ridgeway we paid particular attention to this question. We questioned every respondent about his reading, listening, and study habits, about his educational background and interests, and about his organizational affiliations. In addition we interviewed librarians, educators, and the local distributor of magazines and newspapers.

Television

It is clear from our research that television is by a large margin the single most important source of information on world affairs in Ridgeway. Only 8.9 per cent of the population does not recognize television as an important source of their information. Although they are first likely to learn of an international event or development via television, the few who are well informed, very interested, and more analytical about foreign affairs largely rely on their reading to broaden and deepen their understanding and interpretations of international events because "the television news just hits the high spots except special news programs such as 'Meet the Press' and 'Face the Nation.'"

Eighty-three per cent specify NBC news (channel 10, Columbia, South Carolina) as their primary television source of information. Almost all of these watch the Huntley-Brinkley national network news program, and nearly 41 per cent mentioned the program by name without suggestion from the interviewer. It is possible that the extreme popularity of this program is partially a matter of television reception. Speaking of a competing network's evening news, one viewer reported that "Cronkite doesn't come in very clear." Another said he liked Cronkite better and that Huntley and Brinkley "definitely let their opinions show through." Nevertheless he watched Huntley-Brinkley regularly. In fact CBS (the Cronkite channel) is received primarily from Charlotte (72 miles north) with NBC coming in from Columbia's transmission station (24 miles southeast). However, Ridgeway is located at the highest elevation between the two cities and apparently most residents have a choice of channels. One woman noted with pride that she has the "best TV in Ridgeway and can get all channels." She watches mostly channel 12 from Augusta, Georgia, nearly one hundred miles south. One well educated community leader noted that Huntley and Brinkley have two advantages over Cronkite: there are two of them, and they are in color.[1]

The Huntley-Brinkley program is, in any case, the clear favorite and by far the most important single source of world affairs information. That is not to say that Chet Huntley and David Brinkley are necessarily major influences on Ridgeway's attitudes toward world affairs. There are important differences in the way people react to what they hear. Probably some really do not hear much at all—even if they have the TV on and turned up loud. Those with little or no education probably do not understand much of what is said about international affairs. Those who are strong conservatives probably discount liberal interpretations. Those who are liberals (and we found some, including one who favors Hubert Humphrey for president in 1968) probably dismiss most of the conservative comments reported on the news. But still it is a significant fact that the news of the outside world which reaches Ridgeway on television is exactly the same news which is going

---

[1] In fact both network news programs are in color.

into millions of homes in New York, Philadelphia, and Boston at the same time and in Denver, Chicago, and Los Angeles just a little later.

It has to be concluded that the television news is an important influence in small towns everywhere and is making them less and less different in many respects from big cities everywhere. A sampling of comments by Ridgeway residents describes some of the impact of various television programs. One man who does not like Huntley-Brinkley but listens to them anyway says, "Their prejudices show in their expression, but it's an interesting program." "What prejudice? It's just the news," another responds. One lady noted that she "could hardly let that pass—it's pretty good." Another woman with a ninth-grade education, five children, a two-room shack for a home, and not enough money to buy magazines (which she "would read 'til one o'clock every morning if I had 'em"), patted her television affectionately and said, "David and Chet, that's what I watches." Having only a ninth-grade education, she cannot be called "sophisticated" in her understanding of world affairs, but she listens regularly and she is aware of the broad outlines of major world events. She knows, for example, who the Secretary-General of the United Nations is, but she is quite confused about his role. "He double-crossed America on some policy."

Only three persons interviewed (one Negro and two Whites) reported having no television sets. (One has since received a set as a gift from a relative.) A fair number reported that they watched TV for news because their eyes were too weak to do much reading. Quite a few were emphatic that they watch the news regularly and carefully. One functional illiterate reported that he watches "news and world affairs and nothing else. I don't look at them there pictures." Several people reported that they had no time for television but that the children watch the news and then talk about it at the supper table. Ninety-one per cent watch the TV news.[2] No major event in world politics goes unnoticed in even the poorest or least educated home in Ridgeway. In some it may go pretty much unmentioned. In others it may cause great concern, send one or more members of the family to the newspaper or a magazine for more information, start conversations with friends, eventually result in developing the community's understanding of the processes of international relations.

---

[2] Ridgeway's mayor thinks—and we agree—that there is probably a substantial decline in the summertime viewing of Huntley-Brinkley. The longer days of summer permit fishing and hunting, etc., to later hours.

A few people mentioned the weekly interview program "Meet the Press" and NBCs United Nations correspondent Pauline Frederick (both radio and TV) as sources of their information about world affairs. It is clear, however, that the evening news is the primary television source. We do not harbor any illusions about high correlations between the amount of time spent watching the news and the amount of information acquired in the process. This is not to say that the high viewing rate does no good. We did discover, however, that of fourteen in-town residents who had never heard of the United Nations, nine do watch the news on television. One of these mentioned both "Meet the Press" and Huntley-Brinkley as programs that he watches regularly.

Commenting on the role of television in transforming the Deep South, one writer has noted optimistically that his barber especially enjoyed "That Was the Week That Was" and that the barber "could find much enjoyment and presumably some meaning in the program."[3] Probably the generalization is valid. But our research supports it only with the reservation that "watching" (and even "enjoying" or "approving") is not necessarily "understanding". That, however, is not the note on which we would conclude. Clearly television news—and particularly the Huntley-Brinkley program—is the major source of world affairs information in Ridgeway and, at least partly as a result of this fact, the town is fairly well informed on current international events.

We do not intend to go overboard and recite an idealized version of a small town which deserves an award for remarkably responsible attention to the duties of citizenship. Ridgeway is not the nation's greatest market for serious television roundtables on weighty problems of world politics. What does seem impressive is that the percentage of people in this small town who watch the "Today Show," "Meet the Press," and the "Huntley-Brinkley Report" is not markedly different from that found in any city—north, south, east and west—in this shrinking land of nationwide television networks.[4]

---

[3] Louis D. Rubin, Jr., in *The Deep South in Transformation,* ed. Robert Highsaw (Tuscaloosa; Univ. of Alabama Press, 1964), pp. 156-57.

[4] No figures are available to show how many people, nationally, "usually watch" any of these shows. However, the American Research Bureau for November 1966 reports (in a survey which asked the significantly different question "Are you *now watching?"*) that the national percentages were: "Today," 5 per cent; "Meet the Press," 4 per cent; and Huntley-Brinkley, 19 per cent. For the same month A. R. B. reports the Columbia, South Carolina, figures as 8, 9, and 43.

Our conclusions generally affirm Hero's: "Television has been more responsible for expansion of contacts of the Southern masses with the world than any other medium, and perhaps than all other mass media combined." [5] There is one possible exception. Hero reports that the "more ardent segregationists and traditionalists among those interviewed had largely ceased to view television appearances of . . . Chet Huntley, David Brinkley . . . whom they called 'slanderers of the South' or comparable names." [6] We found only one negative comment about the Huntley-Brinkley program, and the person making that observation continues to watch the program anyway.

Television is rapidly nationalizing the South—including the small towns. In retrospect it seems strange that we could ever have believed that Ridgeway would be markedly different from the national norm. Every aspect of the communications and transportation revolution militates against either regional or rural insularity. The change is rapid and inevitable. The impact is predictable and strong.

Radio

With radio the picture is radically different. Forty-four per cent report that they do not get any world affairs information by radio, and this figure would be over 50 per cent if it did not include the high school students whose listening rate (mostly rock-and-roll stations) is relatively high (80.6 per cent). Many persons report that they do not even own radios. Many who have and use radios say that they just turn them on for music. Apparently the news (which most stations in the area report at least hourly) is "tuned out" by a very large number of listeners. One woman (a college graduate in a comfortable income bracket) says she listens to the "DJ with the beautiful voice." Several whose radios continued to play as a matter of course during the interviews with them said, "No, I don't *listen* [emphasis added] to the radio." To some degree radio seems to be treated simply as background accompaniment to daily life. One man even reported that he sometimes plays the radio and the television simultaneously.

---

[5] *The Southerner and World Affairs* (Baton Rouge, Louisiana State Univ. Press, 1965), p. 47.
[6] Ibid., p. 427.

Newspapers

The daily newspaper is easily the second most important source of world affairs information in Ridgeway. Only 20.4 per cent report that they do not get some world affairs information from the papers. Among the papers the morning Columbia *State* is clearly the most important. Seventy per cent of the people read the *State*. Fifteen per cent (most of them also read the *State*) read the afternoon Columbia *Record*. Nearly 12 per cent (all of whom also read a daily paper) read the nearest local paper, the weekly Winnsboro *News and Herald*. Under 10 per cent read any paper from outside the immediate area.

More than half of those interviewed read the editorials. We were unable to determine their reactions (question was improperly phrased in the early interviews and subsequently dropped all together), but it is clear that the White population was more impressed with the *State's* (generally conservative) editorials than the Negro population. The Winnsboro paper, which is the most liberal of the three, carries no regular international news but does have frequent editorials or feature articles on world affairs. For example, during the period of this survey the *News and Herald* began a long series of interesting articles by a Ridgeway man reporting his experiences during a year in Germany.

As with television and radio it is clear that not all who reported exposure to the source actually partook of the fare. One man admitted, "I looks at the headlines and that's about it—don't fool with the rest of it—a lot of it is not so anyway—politics and all that junk." One woman said she skipped the news but read "editorials, Dennis the Menace, and Abby." Two men simply said they "take the *State* but don't read it." On balance, however, it appears that nearly 80 per cent of the people of Ridgeway see at least the daily headline news about international affairs, and the newspaper rates second only to television as a source of such information.

Again, our findings generally reaffirm Hero, who reports that Southerners tend to be more liberal than their newspapers.[7] While Hero refers to W. D. Workman, editor of the *State*, as "monolithically conservative,"[8] there is some evidence that even the Columbia newspapers are moving to a less isolationist view. Taking note of the governor's proclamation of U.N. Day in 1965, the Co-

---

[7] Ibid., p. 237.
[8] Ibid., p. 418.

lumbia *Record* (the *State-Record* Company's "progressive" after-noon paper) concluded that "but few would quarrel over the stated goals of the world organization and not many will dispute the necessity for U. S. continuance in the body, with a realistic ap-preciation of its strength and shortcomings. The U.N. is no corner-stone of American foreign policy, but it is a valuable building block." [9] The *State* meanwhile has not directly called for U. S. withdrawal, although it is seemingly inclined to a reassessment of U. S. membership if mainland China were seated in the United Nations. (According to Hero's report, only one third of the South would favor withdrawal if mainland China were seated in the United Nations.) [10] Workman himself stops short of calling for withdrawal while stressing the need for study and "fundamental reform" of the organization and preferring, with Herbert Hoover, an organization of "like-minded" states if the "drift away from the Charter" is not reversed.[11]

Our findings also tend to confirm Hero's conclusion that Negroes rarely read editorials.[12] However, the evidence is strong that neither Negroes nor Whites pay major attention to the editorials and that even when they do read the editorials, there is a considerable tendency to disagree or to be suspicious of any newspaper's con-clusions.

Magazines

We do not believe that our findings with respect to magazines as sources of world affairs information are very reliable. There is a tendency for persons who are asked about their magazine read-ing habits to name magazines they see or know about whether or not they read them. And, on the other side, there is a tendency to forget some magazines. For example, one woman said at first, "No, I don't read any magazines." A few minutes later she "remembered" that she "regularly" reads several, including *Reader's Digest* "cover to cover." Our findings are also clouded in this area by the fact that the international content of magazines varies and that the "regu-lar" reader may or may not read such international articles as do appear. We did not attempt to determine reading habits beyond

---

[9] The Columbia *Record*, October 28, 1965, p. 10A, col. 1.
[10] Op. cit., p. 240.
[11] In a telephone conversation with Urban Whitaker, March 31, 1966. See also the *State*, August 21, 1965, p. 8A.
[12] Op. cit., p. 511.

the general questions "Is this magazine a source of world affairs information for you?"

We believe that our findings are fairly accurate with respect to the percentages of those who do not get any world affairs information from magazines. Perhaps the figures indicating which magazines are read reflect with fair accuracy the relative importance of the various publications in Ridgeway.

Our conclusion is that magazines are a relatively minor source of world affairs information except for the handful of well-informed persons who read them regularly for a more detailed understanding of international affairs which were heard about first via television. In terms of the number of subscribers *Reader's Digest* is the most popular single magazine. *Look* and *Life* follow in that order, while *Newsweek* clearly outdistances *Time* and *U. S. News and World Report*. We received very few reports that Negroes read *Ebony, Jet,* or other Negro publications. While this may in part reflect an unwillingness to give such information to White interviewers, we found some confirmation at the local newsstand. The more serious publications do not sell in Ridgeway either to White or Negro readers. Comic books of every variety, fiction, and "true romance" types dominate the newsstand sales. More serious reading is generally received by mail subscriptions, but even so, we found little evidence of such publications as *Saturday Review* (two people mentioned it, and one had already dropped her subscription), *Harper's,* and *The Atlantic.* No one in Ridgeway ever mentioned to us such journals as *The New Republic, The Nation,* or *The Reporter,* and every indication pointed to conservative reading habits. Probably the two most influential magazines in the community are *Reader's Digest* and *U. S. News and World Report*—the former because more people read it, and the latter because more of the town's leaders read and discuss it. The liberalization of the *Saturday Evening Post* in the mid 1960s has not escaped Ridgeway readers—at least two of them have canceled their subscriptions as a result.

Once again our findings agree with Hero's conclusions that Southerners do not read many liberal magazines, are inclined to dislike *Time,* prefer the pictorials *Look* and *Life,* and are much more likely to read magazines if they are college educated.[13]

---

[13] Ibid., pp. 45–46, 254.

Books

Only a small minority of the people of Ridgeway read any books that might even remotely be concerned with world affairs. Most apparently do not read any books at all. It was not uncommon for us to hear "we are not readers in this family" or "we just don't have time to read because we're all so busy." Quite a few reported that they "don't read any more." Some suffered from eyesight problems, but one woman said, "I just don't like modern books." Apparently television has pre-empted such time as may once have been spent on reading.

Hero's estimate that Negroes—as a group in the South—read about one tenth as many books as Whites seems to be supported by our limited findings.[14] However, the more pertinent point is that virtually no one in Ridgeway regularly reads books on world affairs. It may be meaningful that no one even mentioned the Book-of-the-Month Club. Although we did not ask specifically about it, we discussed books and reading habits with someone in 91 per cent of the households in Ridgeway.

Library facilities are relatively good. The Fairfield County Library in Winnsboro is an excellent public facility with twenty-one thousand volumes and a bookmobile service covering the entire county twice monthly. Membership is free. A branch library is maintained in the Century House. Both the main and branch libraries are integrated, but only 155 Negroes are members—about twenty of them in Ridgeway and environs. The library's collection on international affairs is good, but there is not much demand for it. In the main library there are six books on the United Nations for adults and four for children, but none of them has been checked out often. The Winnsboro *News and Herald* and an active library committee have done excellent work in calling public attention to the value of reading books. It is clear that the low reading rate in Ridgeway (and it may be no different from the national average) is a result of low public demand rather than lack of facilities or encouragement.

Travel

Hero asserts that a general lack of intercultural experience is characteristic in the Deep South and particularly in its rural and

---

[14] Ibid., p. 511.

small town areas.[15] While we do not have any basis for comparison with other areas, we can report that only 12.9 per cent of Ridgeway residents have traveled outside the United States, that more than half of those were on military duty, and that some of the remainder have gone only as far as Canada or Mexico. There are, however, signs that the situation is changing. One prominent Ridgeway family was, at the time of the survey, away for a two-year stay in Europe. As we noted above, another prominent resident, recently returned, was publishing a series of articles about his trip in the Winnsboro *News and Herald*. Seventh-graders reported that, although none had been outside the country, most of them want to go and more than one fourth expect to travel abroad during their lifetimes. Both figures were lower in the Geiger (Negro) seventh grade than in the Ridgeway Elementary (integrated) seventh grade.

Fewer than half of all Ridgeway residents have traveled domestically (defined as beyond an adjacent state). Just under 39 per cent reported domestic travel—mostly in the East and Southeast. In response to the question "Have you ever traveled abroad?" one resident answered, "Yes, sir, I've been to Moab, Utah." Among the people of Ridgeway she is indeed one of a minority to have traveled more than a thousand miles from home.

Schools

Among the sources of world affairs information the schoolhouse is the only major one which comes close to equaling television. The schools not only provide a great deal of information through formal study but also encourage the use of such other sources as television, radio, newspapers, periodicals, and books. We found considerable evidence that the influence of the schools flows regularly into the home, particularly via the supper table.

We attended classes at all four of the schools that enroll Ridgeway students—Ridgeway Elementary (integrated, about 100 students, including 17 Negroes); Geiger School (Negro, elementary); Winnsboro High School (integrated); and Fairfield High School (Negro). We talked with principals, with teachers having primary responsibility in the world affairs field, and with librarians. We studied the relevant textbooks.

---

[15] Ibid., p. 61.

For the elementary level there is no county-wide standard curriculum requirement, but most schools follow the same pattern. At Geiger, for example, geography is the subject closest to world affairs, and it is studied by seventh-graders for one period three times a week. The textbook is *Your Country and the World* by Robert Glendinning (Ginn & Co., 1958). Chapter 29 of the book is entitled "The Road Ahead: The Struggle for Peace and Freedom." It describes the United Nations from its origins during World War II to the present and discusses many other international agencies and problems. There were no maps in the classroom (basically a science room) but many in the text. A daily paper was on display, and there were many other visual aids. Although the teacher is trained primarily in science, her presentation was excellent and classroom recitation was very effective. From twelve hundred to fifteen hundred books were on hand for a school library which was to be opened by May 1966. Sufficient funds for a library had not previously been available, but a full-time librarian completed her orientation training and began her work at the school in March 1966.

Ridgeway Elementary School has a small library inherited from the high school which previously had shared the premises. The library is well used, although it cannot be staffed except as an extra assignment for a teacher who already has a full classroom load. The budget is about $1.50 per student. Some high-school students still use the library, but with a base of only about a hundred students it cannot be expected to develop a large selection.

The Fairfield High library has a full-time librarian and several student assistants. It has about five books per student (total about four thousand volumes) and a budget of $1,600 annually. It is open before and after school and has a reading room seating about fifty students.

At Winnsboro High School there are forty-five hundred to forty-eight hundred books (for 813 students, or a little over five per student). Study-hall students keep the library busy most of the time. The full-time librarian is exceptionally able, well trained, and experienced. There is a wide selection of magazines and daily and weekly newspapers. The *Newsweek* "Map of the Month" and other visual education devices are prominently and attractively displayed. The *Newsweek* map is placed "so they can't miss it" and receives a lot of attention.

Both high schools encourage (and in practice really require) students to follow major international developments in the news.

Both of the classes we attended were very well taught—emphasizing the development of each student's thinking on various public issues through reading followed by class reports and discussion. At Winnsboro High the front page of the *State* is required daily reading for the eleventh-grade U. S. history class, which has to be prepared for questions on public affairs every Friday. At Fairfield High students are assigned to read "World Affairs in Perspective" in *Senior Scholastic,* and there is a vigorous class discussion after individual reports.

The high school textbooks are national standard works: *Story of Nations* by Rogers, Adams, and Brown (1962 edition) and *History of a Free People* by Brogden and McCutchen (1964). Both books have competent sections about the United Nations and other world organizations.

While we have not attempted to do a complete survey of the international content of their curricula, we believe that the schools attended by Ridgeway students have adequate facilities and competent instruction. The schools provide the best sources of basic information on world affairs and a strong stimulus to utilize the advantages of the major communications media.

Conversations

We have already made repeated reference to this source of information and do not need to treat it at length. The content of the world affairs information which travels on this circuit is, of course, determined by many other influences. Still it is noteworthy that a substantial number of Ridgeway residents get a substantial amount of their information on world affairs via this second or third-hand source. In particular it is apparent that many busy mothers and wives pick up quite a bit of information from children and husbands at the supper table. We are informed by Hero that the prominent influence of word-of-mouth communication is likewise so throughout the country in small towns, especially among noncosmopolitan majorities. "The lower the level of interest and sophistication in world affairs, the greater the relative impact of . . . the two step flow of communication, that is, from the mass media to the more interested and from them by word of mouth to their relatives, peers, and other face-to-face contacts who are less interested." [16]

---

[16] Letter, May 8, 1966, from Alfred O. Hero, managing editor of *International Organization* (Boston: World Peace Foundation).

On the other hand, some of the ladies active in book groups are sources of information for their families (see below).

Organization

We are not confident that our research has given us either a complete or an accurate idea of the organizational affiliations of the Ridgeway community. We asked everyone we interviewed to name all the organizations to which he or she belongs. No one named the John Birch Society, the NAACP, the Ku Klux Klan, or the Americans for Democratic Action. But with the possible exception of the ADA we would not feel confident in asserting that none of these has a single member in Ridgeway. There are two weaknesses in our information on this subject: first, there are some organizations (such as those just named) in which membership would be unpopular or for other reasons might not be divulged; second, it is likely that most anyone would have difficulty remembering all of his affiliations in answer to a question casually posed during such interviews as those we conducted.

We do note the following from our results: Negroes report very few organizational affiliations (only three memberships were reported by 35 respondents inside the town limits as compared to 113 reported by 96 White respondents); very few residents in any group reported membership in any national organization except Masons and American Legion—and most were inactive even in the local branches of these groups. The most popular local groups are churches (discussed below) and the Women's Club and garden clubs. The Women's Club (a meeting of which we attended) is very active. It has an international relations chairman and occasionally sponsors programs with world affairs content. We cannot comment on the quality of the club's world affairs programs. The meeting we attended featured an excellently presented program on the quality, requirements, and anticipated contribution of the community's new nursing home for the elderly. However, we are inclined to think that the international relations committee is the least active and that the club has only minimal influence on the community's world affairs thinking. On rare occasions world affairs books are reviewed; and the club has among its membership one who is capable—but shy—of giving such reviews. The club rarely if ever has experts coming in from the University of South Carolina or Columbia College to give world affairs lectures. The club emphasizes books, and its monthly meetings probably are the major vehicle of serious conversation in Ridgeway. The membership and attendance are not limited to the town limits but reach as far as Blythewood (eight miles) and Winnsboro. There are no Negro members.

Ninety-four per cent of the Ridgeway residents are church members. About ninety per cent of these are Baptists or Presbyterians. We talked with all of the ministers of Ridgeway's three White and three Negro churches. We attended services at the three churches within the town limits. Generally it is true that church-affiliated groups are the most active organizations in Ridgeway—although nearly all the ministers are concerned about the level of support given by nominal members. Most of the churches—and particularly the Negro churches—do not attempt to do very much (beyond their mission work) about world affairs. International subjects are rarely topics for sermons, and there are few discussion group meetings devoted to world affairs. However, Ridgeway's ministers all agree that the church has a role in communicating information about world affairs and in assisting its people in thinking about such problems as ethics and foreign policy. And they all try to stay fairly well abreast of "what's going on in the world."

One of the town's ministers thinks "the church has an obligation to teach people how to get along without war because the church is a peaceable institution and should inculcate a love for peace in the people and keep telling the people to advocate peace and keep peace." But it is hard to interest the people with this subject "unless they have boys and girls in or about to join the army."

Another of Ridgeway's ministers emphasizes prayer for "peace," "the President in the discharge of his international responsibilities," and "the people of all nations." But this minister does not formally discuss world affairs problems at church gatherings in spite of his personal belief that "the church has an obligation as a worldwide concern to address itself to problems of international relations." His excuse for not making an affirmative response to this belief is "limited time." Since his church is "really a part-time church because it has no Sunday night service or mid-week prayer service during the summer months," he must use what time they have together for "evangelistic messages and messages dealing with the spiritual welfare of man." His reason for not doing as he believes is fear of insufficient congregational interest and support. "Membership in the large big-city churches tends to divide along lines of education and social class. But all groups and classes are represented in our small church; and whereas the well-educated would listen with interest and approval, others would feel that the pulpit should not be used for the discussion of world affairs."

Another minister—with a fresh and inquiring mind—"definitely feels" that world affairs are a relevant concern of the church. "If Christ is Lord, he is Lord of the whole world; and the church cannot segregate itself from the world, or else it is not the body of Christ." However, it is not the practice of this young minister to discuss world affairs problems from the pulpit. He thinks "place is important." "The best place is in Sunday School, where it can be dialogue—it must be a dialogue." Two such dialogues were conducted at the church during the first six months of his pastorate. The first one was an educational discussion about communism for the high-school group within the church membership. The second was also a young peoples' discussion group on the problems of Christian ethics. The discussion dealt with such questions as the morality of the war in Viet Nam, pacifism, and draft-card burning. Despite these beginning efforts this hard-working, dedicated servant of the church feels that "the church has no real impact on the community's world affairs attitudes—and that's awful."

Generally we conclude that the churches are not a major source of international information or a major direct influence on attitudes about world affairs. Our conclusions again tend to support Hero's observation about the South as a whole. He concludes that "in fact most organizations sponsoring discussion [on world affairs] in the South have operated only in the white community." [17] While he noted that "churches have been the social and communication centers of Southern Negro life to an even greater degree than among Southern whites," he believes that the churches' "impact on Negro thinking in the field of foreign affairs, with notable exceptions, has been minimal." [18]

His conclusions are similar for White churches, whose ministers he believes have "only rather limited influence on thinking about world affairs" and because "local inertia and opposition" are formidable, have "gradually curtailed their attention to international developments." [19]

[17] *The Southerner and World Affairs*, p. 515.
[18] Ibid., p. 516.
[19] Ibid., p. 451.

None

Finally we take brief note of those for whom the answer to the question about sources of international affairs is "none." Nearly 10 per cent of those we interviewed, for example, had never heard of the United Nations. According to Hero, "the 10 per cent who never heard of the U.N. seems a bit high contrasted with the South in general." [20] But this difference cannot be explained—even in part —by the relatively high percentage of Negroes in the area. The breakdown of responses shows almost no significant variations according to race. The one exception was that no Negroes opposed the United Nations. Slightly more Negroes than Whites either gave no opinion or had never heard of the United Nations. The factor which correlated with ignorance, however, was illiteracy rather than race. All of the "never heard of it" category (10.7 per cent of total) and most of the "don't know enough to say" group (28.2 per cent) were functional illiterates, White or Negro. We are forced to conclude that at least a recognizable segment of the population simply does not absorb any information about world affairs even when exposed to it. Most of this group did not go beyond the third grade in school, reads nothing, participates in no organizational activity except the church, and automatically "tunes out" such radio and television news as comes into the home. We can make only a rough comparison between the size of this "know nothing" group in Ridgeway and national figures for ignorance of the U.N.[21] We know that the group exists. But we know that it is small, and we do not believe that it will survive the growing educational opportunities available to today's children.

---

[20] Letter from Hero, op. cit.

[21] In most national polls about the United Nations the combined total of "no opinion" and "don't know" is about 10 per cent and often is less.

IV

RIDGEWAY'S ATTITUDES TOWARD
THE UNITED NATIONS AND THE FUTURE

We asked four primary questions about the attitudes of Ridgeway citizens toward: the United Nations, the likelihood of another world war, their personal future, and the shape of the world in the year 2000 A.D. In each category we asked a number of subquestions designed to increase our understanding of the attitudes expressed. We are confident that our results on these questions are an accurate reflection of the attitudes in Ridgeway as of 1965–66. In almost all cases the respondents were very friendly and cooperative and, we believe, generally candid. These questions—the primary reason for the interview—came close to the end of each conversation after good rapport was established and most of the initial fears about the interview had been erased. The results are generally very encouraging to those who believe in the United Nations and, we believe, describe a process of change which is very rapidly erasing regional differences in American attitudes toward world affairs. In our conclusions we will return briefly to the question. As we proceed we will make comparison of our result for Ridgeway with those reported by Charles Lerche and Alfred Hero for the South in general.

The United Nations

After recording personal data and talking with the respondent about his views concerning the future in general and world war in particular (both reported below), we asked, "What do you think of the United Nations?" Depending on the response we continued the conversation far enough to be sure in our own minds which of six categories accurately described the respondent's view: strongly favorable; tending to be favorable; neutral; tending to oppose; strongly opposed; never heard of the United Nations. The biggest problem was to separate "neutral" from "never heard of it." We tried to resolve the problem with questions designed to make it quite clear whether the respondent knew anything at all about the organization. For example, "Who is the Secretary-General?" "Where is the U.N.?" "What do you think of Ambassador Goldberg's work?" etc. We are quite confident that the "never heard of it" category is accurately tabulated.

The neutral category is more questionable. We are sure that it includes some who simply have not any opinion—in most cases because they know very little about it. However, it probably also includes some who have opinions but for various reasons did not choose to divulge them. This is likely to be true for quite a few Negro respondents who as a group showed more reluctance than Whites to give their opinions. Hero reported, "As one would anticipate, Negroes have been more inclined than whites to reply 'don't know' or 'no opinion.'"[1] However, the spread between White (27.1 per cent) and Negro (31.4 per cent) "neutrals" in the town limits is not exceptionally high.

In an extended comment about the "no opinion" in the South, Hero indicated that those offering no opinion are, when pushed further on the matter, "inclined" more to be disapproving of international commitments than are those who do offer opinions. He also notes that on general questions like "whether or not we should stay in the U.N.," the "no opinion" group among Southern adults has been typically small—under one fifth.[2] We found it to be slightly higher (24.4 per cent over-all), and when the "never heard of it" category is combined with the "no opinion" category, the total was slightly more than one third (33.9 per cent).

Strongly favorable 29.4%
Tend to be favorable 32.1%

Total favorable 61.5%

---

[1] Alfred O. Hero, *The Southerner and World Affairs* (Baton Rouge: Louisiana State Univ. Press, 1965), p. 504.
[2] Ibid., p. 57.

Strongly opposed 0.4%
Tend to be opposed.....   4.2%

Total opposed 4.6%

No opinion or neutral....   24.4%
Never heard of it........   9.5%

Total no opinion 33.9%

100.0%

With respect to the other four categories we believe our findings are accurate and meaningful. In most cases the respondent himself chose the term describing his general feeling. Combining the "strongly favorable" and "tends to be favorable" groups (29.4 per and 32.1 per cent respectively), we found that 61.5 per cent of all those interviewed are favorable toward the United Nations. Combining the two "opposing" categories (0.4 per cent and 4.2 per cent), we get a grand total of only 4.6 per cent expressing general opposition to the United Nations.

The question was general. Many of those favoring the U.N. have specific reservations or are critical of particular situations such as the refusal of the French and the Russians to pay the Congo assessment. There are some who support it but out of religious convictions feel that "it's fighting a losing battle." This is the view of one of Ridgeway's ministers who, "looking at it from the standpoint of Jesus Christ," says "there will be no peace until there is peace in the heart, and there will be no peace in the heart until God is there." The minister's view is shared by another "strong supporter" of the U.N. belonging to a different denomination who argues that "the U.N. is definitely a necessary thing. It has prevented an all-out war up until now. However, it will never achieve its ultimate aim which is to bring peace to the world because the Bible says it won't. I can't tell you the book, chapter, and verse, but it says peace will come only with the second coming of Christ." Several other respondents indicated that they share the same view.

It is also quite clear that Ambassador Adlai Stevenson's performance at the U.N.—particularly his tough stand during the Security Council's debate of the 1962 Cuban missile crisis—added something to Ridgeway's appreciation of the United Nations. A number of respondents—including one who hadn't heard of his death and wished to see him run for president in 1968—paid tribute to Stevenson's outstanding statesmanship. "Stevenson was an out-standing statesman and representative of the U. S. at the United Nations. He stood up to the Russians and told them off when they got unruly. I believe he would have told them some more if he had just got more backing."

Most of those expressing opposition qualified their positions with such remarks as "If carried out right, it would be a good thing"; "I would say the U.N. would be the greatest organization in the world if it were doing what it was designed to do"; "I reckon it has pre-vented something fearful"; "As originally conceived it was a good thing and could be useful if all countries paid their part." One of those who "tends to oppose" the U.N. but nevertheless acknowl-edges the world organization's notable achievements "feels it has done some good in some places but I don't think the U.S. can buy other nations' friendship. It has not proved effective in stopping small wars such as we have in Viet Nam, but in some other places it has proved to be an effective force."

When pressed further on the specific question of whether the U.S. should continue membership in the U.N., only three (of 272 interviewed) wanted the U. S. to get out. The one person "strongly opposed" to the U.N. said her reason was "to [sic] many for the other side," and she would have the U. S. get out "because they [the U.N.] want to be boss." More typical of those expressing oppo-sition was another lady who concluded that "we can't afford to get out. Better be in there knowing what they're doing."

The reasons offered for being favorable toward the United Na-tions were numerous. A few noted among their reasons for support that it "helps bring food and clothing to people, especially chil-dren, who are starving." But the two most common were its work for peace (17.2 per cent of all respondents) and its value as a com-munications device (13.7 per cent). Representative of the two most commonly given reasons for favoring the U.N. are the remarks of a woman who "strongly favors" the U.N. because "it plays a part in keeping the peace. Just knowing it's there has some influence for peace. It gives me a little reassurance to know that we're still trying; and I would be very much disturbed to see it disbanded or disorganized or more disorganized"; and those of a man "strongly favorable" to the U.N. because it "would be a good thing if people could sit at a table and peacefully settle problems without shoot-ing at one another. You can't settle any problem without talking about it and many problems will disappear once those who disagree or dislike one another sit down and talk and learn to know each other."

The twelve who oppose the U.N. mentioned a variety of reasons, including excessive cost to the U.S., overrepresentation of new nations, and "it doesn't do anything." Only one person complained that the U.N. is dominated by communism. So far as we are able to tell, there is no evidence to justify the conclusion that there is "evidence at every hand of . . . paranoid patriotism where the extreme Rightwingers have simply substituted the abominable Commie for the abominable Yankee." [3] Such generalization—possibly accurate in describing fringe groups—should always be judged alongside the fact that they refer to a tiny minority. There is an unfortunate temptation to generalize about the South (and other areas such as Texas, Berkeley, and Southern California) on the basis of loud noises made by small numbers.

We firmly believe that the accurate generalization about "Ridgeway and the United Nations" is that the people of this town support U. S. membership in the U.N. because it is practical and a hope for peace to keep in close and continuous communication with all the peoples of the world—communists included. There are at least three in Ridgeway, and probably more, who count the world body so important that they would favor, if necessary to its survival, the U.S. bearing an "unfair" part of its operational costs. One of these gentlemen—a traditionalist Southern conservative who "would vote for Strom Thurmond for anything he runs for"— says, "I don't like the failure of others to pay dues but the U.N. is worth our paying a bit more than our fair share." A retired businessman who politically calls himself "an independent for Strom Thurmond" feels that "if the United Nations' existence is dependent upon the U. S. bearing a disproportionate share of its financial burdens, then I would support our doing so."

The third Ridgeway resident openly taking a stand this strong in support of the U.N. is also a prosperous businessman who describes himself as a "Jeffersonian, middle-of-the-road Southern Democrat who is no follower of Thurmond." This gentleman, who is one of the town's better-educated and more articulate people, thinks "nations should be made to pay assessments against them. But if forcing them to pay would destroy the U.N., then I would

---

[3] Ernest M. Lander, Jr., in *The Deep South in Transition*, ed. Robert Highsaw (Tuscaloosa: Univ. of Alabama Press, 1964), p. 138, commenting on the findings of Betty Chamj as reported in *The Atlantic*, November 1962.

support the U.S. in carrying the load because the U.N. is our last best hope. Nations must learn to compromise their differences. The U.S. can't have its way in all things." We even found one prominent citizen who firmly believes that the United Nations should be the vehicle for developing a world government which "we must have if we are not going to destroy ourselves."

Perhaps our belief that Ridgeway's attitudes toward the United Nations are about the same as those of most other Americans is the central conclusion of our study. While it may be surprising to many people (in fact it was to us), it does not vary significantly from the findings reported regularly by pollsters and other investigators of Southern attitudes on world affairs in recent years. Below we list conclusions from the two major works on this subject (Lerche and Hero) and compare them with our findings.[4]

Lerche, pp. 244–45, 263

"The list of the enemies of the South is long and tends to vary with the tactical needs of the moment, but it has recently always included Presidents Eisenhower and Kennedy, Chief Justice Warren, the NAACP . . . the Secretary-General of the United Nations. . . ."

"The three multilateralist aspects of current American policy that draw the sharpest fire from Southern demagoguery are the United Nations, foreign aid and American policy toward the emerging nations. . . ."

Comment

Lerche qualifies his comment as a report of the line spouted by demagogues who talk to the poor Whites. In our opinion this is an extremely meaningful qualification which restricts the application of the remarks to an increasingly small minority whose influence—admittedly significant beyond its numbers — is also diminishing.

Lerche, p. 105, reports the U. S. House of Representatives vote in favor of the U. N. Bond Issue as follows:

We take note of three things: first, the South still voted in favor, if by a much smaller majority than the two coasts; sec-

[4] All quotations are from Charles O. Lerche, *The Uncertain South: Its Changing Patterns of Politics in Foreign Policy* (Chicago: Quadrangle Press, 1964), or Hero, *The Southerner and World Affairs.*

Entire House	251–134	65.2%
South	63–53	54.3%
Midwest	61–50	54.9%
Two Coasts	127–31	80.4%

ond, the issue is not simply to favor or not favor the U. N. but to support a particular means of financing a particular operation; third, there may be significant differences between the public view and the congressman's view on issues which are not top-priority matters to a majority of voters.

Hero, p. 368

". . . by 1962 Southerners who . . . had basically favorable views of Senator Goldwater were considerably more apt to feel the U. N. was doing a poor job, that we should withdraw from the U. N. . . ."

Hero, p. 402

"Most Deep Southern whites who would withdraw from the U. N. were very conservative on race, but the majority of strong segregationists would continue our membership."

We found that all those in Ridgeway who oppose the U. N. were in favor of Senator Goldwater in the 1964 presidential election. But we note that of 57 in-town residents who favored Goldwater, only 10 expressed opposition to the U. N. We believe that Hero's second comment (p. 402) is more significant than his first. The most important point is that most Southerners do not want the U. S. to withdraw from the U. N.

Hero, pp. 505, 521, 529

"Southern Negroes have been as or more conservative than Southern Whites (on multilateralist international thinking)." "The differences have typically been large: a majority of Negroes replying has often advised that we 'stay out' whereas a majority of Southern Whites has always recommended that we 'take an active part.'" "Negroes have been no more favorable toward the U. N. in general than whites."

Our findings in Ridgeway are in marked contrast to these conclusions. We did not talk to a single Negro who opposed or tended to oppose the United Nations. While the total percentage of Negroes in favor of the U. N. is lower than among Whites, the figures are reversed when the "never heard of it" category is eliminated.

Hero, pp. 549, 241

". . . The growth of approval (for the U. N. after 1953) in the South has been somewhat smaller than in the rest of the country. . . ." "However, differences in thinking about the U. N. between the regions in 1962 were small except where Negro-white disputes were salient. Large majorities in the South felt in 1962 that we should remain in the U. N. and try to make it a success, and a majority of those venturing opinions recommended that we remain in the organization even if Communist China were admitted." ". . . Compared with foreign aid, the U. N. as a general symbol has fared rather well in the South. Whereas the former has been losing supporters during the decade prior to 1963, Southern approval of the U. N. has remained steady or even increased in most respects."

We stand strong with Hero in asserting that a majority of those venturing opinions on U. S. membership in the United Nations recommend that we remain in the organization even if Communist China were admitted. Additional solid support for this assertion is provided by A. T. Steele's *The American People and China* (New York: McGraw Hill, 1966), p. 102: "There are those on the far right in the country who advocate U. S. withdrawal from the United Nations if Communist China is voted in over American objections. Is this view shared by the general public? Emphatically not. When SRC [Survey Research Center, University of Michigan] sought public reaction to this question, 75 per cent of those questioned said the United States should remain in the U. N. even if Communist China is admitted. Only five per cent favored withdrawal." Ridgeway's reaction to this question is in line with the national norm. A majority in Ridgeway still think that it would be better to keep Communist China out of the United Nations. However, a large majority (5 to 1) believe that the United States should remain in the United Nations even if China is seated over American objections. One of our respondents who "tends to oppose" the United Nations nevertheless recommends that we stay even if Communist China is seated because "it is better to be on the inside knowing what is going on than on the outside guessing." Another of our respondents—voicing what probably is the majority opinion in Ridgeway—feels "we should stay in but if possible we definitely should keep them out. Because Nationalist China is recognized as China to me. Red China is a bastard nation ruled by Communist leaders who overthrew said government in China that we now recognize. If we recognize Free China, I do not see how we can recognize Red China. And since I feel that Chiang's China lost the war because of our bungling, I feel that we should support Nationalist China as we now support South Korea, South Viet Nam, etc. In other words, what the heck are we supporting? And do we help by feeding, recognizing, and otherwise nourishing that which continues to bite us?" There are some in Ridgeway who favor an active U. S. effort to seat mainland China in the United Nations. Among them is one who argues that "Red China is a Communist country and should be recognized as such, accepted as such, and admitted to the U.N. because we can better handle them there. As things

now stand, we have no communications with them except
through another government.
They are, after all, the third
most powerful country in the
world. They exist!" While we
have not studied attitudes on
foreign aid and do not have a
current and comparable U.N.
support figure for other regions
of the United States, we are
firmly in agreement with the
conclusion that the "U.N. as a
general symbol has fared rather
well." In Ridgeway 61.5 per cent
of all citizens generally favor it.
And of those who expressed any
opinion at all the support figure
is 93 per cent! [5]

Southerners have long complained that there is as much anti-
Southern prejudice in the North and West as there is anti-Negro
prejudice in the South. We are inclined to agree. As the quotations
and comments above clearly show, there is a wide gap between the
idea—widely held—that the South is strongly opposed to the
United Nations and the reality which polls consistently reveal. Not
only does the rest of the country have an inaccurate view of the
South, but there is good evidence that Southern city-dwellers have
a somewhat distorted view of their small-town neighbors.

A major misconception is that Deep Southern small towns are
hotbeds of anti-U.N. sentiment. On the contrary, as regional polls
have consistently shown and as our research suggests, small towns
in the South—and probably everywhere—are just as much in tune
with reality and therefore favorably disposed toward the United
Nations as are their urban neighbors. In fact, it is likely that Chicago, Dallas, and Los Angeles harbor more anti-U.N. activists than
does the whole Southern countryside.

[5] A general poll conducted by the American Institute of Public Opinion in
1963 showed the following response to the question "How important do you
think it is that we try to make the United Nations a success—very important,
fairly important, or not so important?": very important, 79 per cent; fairly
important, 8 per cent; not so important, 4 per cent; no opinion, 8 per cent; no
response, 1 per cent.

It is not difficult to find evidences of these misconceptions. They are common. In fact (as noted above) the first evidence we found of misconceptions about the international attitudes of Southern townspeople was in ourselves. But we wanted harder evidence, so we developed a questionnaire to measure some common assumptions about U.N. attitudes in Deep Southern small towns. We asked 100 undergraduate students of international relations at San Francisco State College what they thought we would find in a study of attitudes toward the U.N. in Ridgeway, South Carolina. We asked 75 international studies undergraduates at the University of South Carolina the same set of questions. Only about one third (39.0 per cent) of the California students thought that as much as a majority of White residents in a small South Carolina town would tend to favor rather than oppose the United Nations. Nearly twice as many South Carolina students (63.5 per cent) expected that we would find generally favorable attitudes toward the United Nations. Even among the South Carolina students, however, there was a majority who expected that small-town attitudes toward the U.N. would be more conservative than their own. One third (33.9 per cent) of the South Carolina students thought that the predominant attitude in Ridgeway would be opposed to the United Nations.

Both the South Carolina group and the California group expected that a large proportion of Negroes would have no opinion. The South Carolina students overestimated and the California students underestimated the ignorance and noncommitment of Negroes. The California students were close in their estimate of Negro support for the U.N., while the South Carolina students underestimated it (see Table E of Appendix III).

We have found further evidence of both Northern and Southern misconceptions about the level of small town support for the U.N. as we have reported our findings to friends and colleagues. Most often their reaction is that something must be wrong with our survey. We do not think so. We believe that the relevant question is: what is wrong with their impressions? Why do so many Americans —and why did we—develop the mistaken notion that small-town Southerners would likely oppose the United Nations? We think there are at least five primary reasons: (1) the prevalence of anti-U.N. editorials in newspapers, (2) the confusion of anti-integration sentiment with anti-U.N. feelings, (3) the expectation of lower than average information and education levels in small towns, (4) an unhealthy dose of misunderstanding (if not outright prejudice) about the South in the rest of the country, and (5) the fact that opposition even by small numbers makes more headlines than support even by large numbers. We suspect also that it is very easy to overestimate the size of a small minority which makes loud and well-financed noises. As much as they may deserve the fire which is leveled at them, the right-wing extremists probably excite a great deal more opposition than is justified either by their small numbers or by their irrational propositions. Finally we often find it assumed that if successful political candidates are mouthing anti-U.N. slogans, it is therefore proof that their constituents are opposed to the United Nations.

In fact, the politicians may simply be making the same mistakes that others make—believing that the newspapers and the loud extremists reflect public opinion. Other writers have concluded (and our studies support their conclusions) that newspapers generally are more conservative than their readers.[6] And congressmen or presidential candidates may with impunity totally fail to reflect the voter's preferences on other issues (even important ones like the U.N.) as long as they qualify on vital emotional issues such as the race relations questions. For example, we found that Goldwater won over Johnson among Ridgeway Whites solely because Goldwater voted against the 1964 civil rights legislation. Neither Goldwater's feelings nor Strom Thurmond's feeling about the United Nations are well known in Ridgeway. But Thurmond is (and Goldwater was) popular and could probably carry a large majority in Ridgeway even if he opposed the United Nations. It is probably not a significant factor in elections either for local or national offices. The U.N. is simply not a high priority issue in Ridgeway. (Is it in any American community?) But the majority of the citizens in this small Deep Southern town know something about the United Nations and strongly approve of U.S. membership and believe that the world organization is an important force for peace.

In conclusion about "The South and the U.N." we would offer the following observations concerning the widespread belief that Southerners tend to oppose the United Nations. First, so much comment has been made about the minority that does oppose the U.N. that there is an unfortunate tendency to miss the first three words of the valid generalization that "among Southern demagogues, the U.N. is an enemy of the South." Second, so many comparisons have been made between the South and other regions that

---

[6] See Hero, op. cit., p. 377.

there is an unfortunate tendency to miss the first four words of the sometimes valid generalization that "Compared with other regions there is less support for the U.N. in the South." Third, many comparisons have been made between the characteristically internationalist Southern congressional delegation which supported Wilsonianism in the 1920s and the more often divided Southern representatives who were only 63–53 in favor of the U.N. bond issue in the early 1960s. There is an unfortunate tendency to de-emphasize the first few words in the sentence "There has been a decrease in Southern support for multilateralist policies in the past twenty years."

In the limited area of our study there is evidence to give some support to each of these three generalizations. Yet they are more valid than they are relevant. We are convinced that it is both valid and relevant to conclude that the people of Ridgeway, South Carolina, are strong supporters of the United Nations. Leaning more on Hero's research than on our own, we believe that the same can be said of the Deep South as a region.

War

We asked all respondents whether they thought the involvement of the U. S. in another major war was probable, possible, or unlikely. We tabulated the responses in these three categories plus a fourth—no opinion. For those believing a war is probable or possible (and for some of those in the "unlikely" category) we also tabulated responses to the questions "with whom?" and "when?"

Our results on these questions are somewhat clouded. In the first place the term "major war" was ill chosen. "World war" would have been better, as a number of the respondents considered Viet Nam to be a major war. We were inconsistent in asking the "when" question and have not even tabulated those results.[7]

Generally our findings are that the expectation of war runs fairly low. A fraction, about 26 per cent of the total (exactly 25 per cent of Whites inside the town limits), believe that war is probable. About half as many (14.5 per cent) believe that it is unlikely, while 41.6 per cent say "possible." Probably a majority of the "possible"

---

[7] We put a very high value on informality and made sure that all of our contacts were "conversations" rather than "interviews" in the eyes of the respondents. Since we were not rigorously using a detailed questionnaire, some minor questions such as this one were asked too infrequently to support firm conclusions.

do not really expect a big war (complete results are tabulated in Table C of the Appendix).

High-school students' opinions varied considerably from those of their parents. More high-school students (25 per cent) thought war probable and fewer (only 11.1 per cent) thought it unlikely. High-school boys by a majority of 77 per cent expect to be called into military service (but not necessarily in wartime).

Over-all the expectation is that Russia rather than China (13.4 per cent to 12.6 per cent) would be the opponent in a major war. Within the town limit (the most sophisticated and best-educated group), however, the Whites consider China (18.7 per cent to 11.5 per cent) the more likely opponent. Most Negroes expecting future U. S. involvement in a major war named Russia as the likely opponent. However, in the category of nonresident Negroes who work in Ridgeway (predominantly Geiger Elementary teachers) no one named Russia, while 7.1 per cent consider China the likely opponent.

Our findings in this area are at variance with Hero's. He reports not only that Southerners have been less optimistic than other Americans but also that the percentage of Southerners expecting another world war within twenty-five years has been under 50 per cent only once since 1945 (46 per cent in 1961).[8] Although one might expect our 1965–66 findings to show some change, reflecting the cold-war thaw of the last few years, it is also true that this survey was conducted during a period of continuously mounting tension over Viet Nam.

With respect to the Negro tendency to say "don't know" more often than Whites, Hero notes that on questions like "Do you expect a world war with the Communist powers in the next ten years?" Negroes are more likely to approach Whites in the number who do offer opinions.[9] Our findings do not agree. Sixty per cent of the Negroes in town (and nearly 50 per cent of all the Negroes interviewed) declined to state an opinion on this question, while only 12 per cent of the Whites declined. However, the correlation is with lack of education rather than with race. This is clearly shown when the figures are compared with those tabulated for Negroes working in but not living in Ridgeway. This group, which included a significantly large group of well-educated Negro teachers (mostly from Columbia) showed only 35 per cent "no opinion."

[8] Hero, op. cit., pp. 105–7.
[9] Ibid., p. 509.

Responses on this question are particularly important as indicators of the degree to which the small Southern town is joining—or has joined—the national mainstream of thinking on world affairs. It is generally held by the experts that people who are most in tune with contemporary thinking have shifted their concern from Russia, bogeyman of the forties and fifties, to China—the power to fear in the future. In fact, we have found some writers who flatly state that small towns are likely to be behind their big-city neighbors and still think that Russia is the prime threat.

Ridgeway fits the national pattern fairly well. With the single exception of in-town Negroes all the groups we interviewed thought that China poses a greater threat than the Soviet Union. The extent to which Russia is viewed by some in Ridgeway as a people desirous of peace shows clearly in the observation of one in-town Ridgeway resident who believes that "the U.S.S.R. desperately desires peace and will go to almost any extreme to avoid war. She will go farther than the U. S. in an attempt to avoid war —a fact demonstrated by the Cuban missile crisis." Again, the correlation is clearly with education rather than with race. In fact, the most sophisticated response (that is, China poses the greater threat) was among nonresident Negro employees (that is, the group with the highest percentage of college graduates). Throughout our study the pattern is consistent. Education rather than race is the major factor dividing the people of Ridgeway into two groups on most questions about world affairs.

Over-all, our findings show that Ridgeway is much closer to the national average on all these questions than the common stereotype of a Deep Southern small town. There are two possible reasons for this. One is that Ridgeway is better educated and more culturally advantaged than the average town. The other is that many people underrate the South in general and the small towns of the South in particular. If Ridgeway is representative, the truth is—much as it may startle most Northerners and some city-dwelling Southerners—that the small towns are just about as educated and sophisticated as the rest of us.

The Future

We asked two sets of questions about the future. First, we tried to rate each person on a four-point scale from strong optimism to strong pessimism about his own personal future. Then we tried, using the same scale, to rate each one's view of the world in the year 2000 A.D. We also inquired into the reasons for optimism and pessimism.

Our results showed a marked contrast between the short-range personal scale and the long-range (2000 A.D.) expectations. Ridgeway is very optimistic about the immediate future (61.5 per cent optimism, 16.4 per cent pessimism, and 22.1 per cent no opinion). Among the Whites the optimism is two to one; among the Negroes it is three to one or better. Of the fourteen Negroes (mostly school-teachers) who live outside but work in Ridgeway, all were optimists.

Looking toward the year 2000 A.D., however, the total optimism is down (from 61.5 per cent to 43.5 per cent) and the pessimism is up (from 16.4 per cent to 22.9 per cent). The increased pessimism is almost entirely among Whites. White in-town residents who are optimistic (54 per cent against only 27 per cent pessimistic) about their short-range personal future are pessimistic (40 per cent against only 28 per cent optimistic) about their children's future at the turn of the next century. The children, however, disagree. The White teen-agers are, like their parents, happier about the next few years (86 per cent as against only 3 per cent pessimistic) than about the next century. But the children are still optimistic about the long-range future (53 per cent as against only 15 per cent pessimistic).

We cannot say very much about the reasons for these feelings because there were large numbers who offered no reason at all, and those who did give reasons gave so many different ones that a tabulation has little statistical meaning. We do make the following observations. Only thirty (including some repeats) of 272 respondents mentioned race relations as a reason for either optimism or pessimism. Perhaps in part this low figure reflects an unwillingness to comment and consequently does not reflect the real feelings either of Negroes or of Whites. One elderly Negro who obviously bases his hope for a better future on improved race relations believes that "if the President can keep going, it will be a good world to live in. He is ducking nothing and doing all the things Kennedy started, which is just wonderful." A young White man looking ahead to the year 2000 feels it will be "better in a lot of ways, such as new medicines," but it will be worse in other ways, noting that "we'll probably have four or five nigger presidents by then."

While race relations cannot be discounted as a major influence on Ridgeway's thoughts concerning its long-range future, neither

can education and economics. Both are very vital factors in Ridgeway's long-range thinking about the future (and, of course, not
totally unrelated to race). Sixty-one (twice as many as mentioned
race) cited economic conditions as reasons for optimism (37) or
pessimism (24). Again, some were repeats, citing this reason both
for short-range personal future and the next century outlook. Both
White and Negro citizens strongly believe that education is a key
to the future. Nearly 50 per cent of the high school students (eighth
through twelfth grade) are planning to go to college. More probably will. Particularly among older Negroes we heard time and
again the happy prediction that their children and grandchildren
would have better lives because they are getting more and better
education.

A small (about 5 per cent) but determined group of both Whites
and Negroes is thoroughly pessimistic about the future on the
grounds that a general moral decay has set in. We heard some long
and heartfelt lectures particularly about a breakdown in family
discipline. One lady expressed this fear by saying, "We are
so broad-minded. The things they are teaching young people! I
feel sort of fearful for the next few years. Homes have gotten so
lax, so they don't have any discipline. There is disregard of author-
ity. It's too lax. Everything goes; if you can get by with it, it's O.K."

One of Ridgeway's ministers (the others probably agree with
him) feels that we face a future of which a significant part is already determined and knowable. He indicated this feeling with
the assertion that he is "one of those Christians who believes in
the second coming of Jesus Christ. This gears a lot of my thinking.
The Bible says soon and he can come any time. I live one day at
a time trying to project maybe a year." Several in Ridgeway made
remarks evincing agreement with the minister.

We have found in the literature two fairly common reports with
which to compare our findings. Ernest Lander, echoing the conclusion of many writers, describes the old Negro Southerner as "ever
tractable, forgiving, optimistic about the future.[10] We found a significant correlation between race and optimism—especially for the
young and for the better educated. We attribute it, however, to a
realistic view of future developments rather than to anything in-
herent in race or environmental to "old Negro Southerners."

Hero reports 1951 and 1962 surveys about "life" or "things" in
the future in which a majority of Southerners replied "worse" or

---

[10] *The Deep South in Transition,* p. 139.

"about the same." [11] For Whites and for the longer-range future we tend to agree. But we are impressed that in Ridgeway, at least, when they think of their own future in the next few years, even the Whites are optimistic by a large majority. When they contrast this world with the world of the next two or three generations, the Whites are (though in no case by as many as 50 per cent) more pessimistic. To a considerable degree the pessimism is economic. There is a strong minority which, though generally enjoying today's prosperity, cannot believe that it will last. Oddly enough, those who have the least are the most hopeful, and those who have the most are the most fearful. Perhaps Hero is right that "acceptance by perhaps most Southerners of the Calvinistic emphasis on original sin and their intimate contact with racial inequality, poverty, and violence [with which Ridgeway has virtually no experience] have reinforced the impacts of Southern tradition and experiences of an agrarian people, producing the rather general view that evil and guilt are everywhere." [12]

[11] Op. cit., p. 345.
[12] Ibid., p. 346.

V

CONCLUSIONS

Throughout our report we have recorded and described our conclusions. In Tables A to E of Appendix III we have tabulated those of our findings which can be reduced to statistics. In summary and final conclusion, we offer the following observations.

There are strong forces in motion—educational and technological —which will improve the discharge by the people of Ridgeway of those international responsibilities which befall them as citizens of the American democracy. Of the four criteria which Hero identifies for proper popular participation in democratic government (interest, information, realistic analysis, and action),[1] we find that Ridgeway is stronger on the first three and weaker on the fourth. We feel that our findings—as already reported above—strongly indicate that Ridgeway's 397 citizens have about the same level of interest and much the same kind of contact with the ouside world as most Americans, North and South, rural and urban. We believe also that our findings show Ridgeway's citizens to be by and large the possessors of an appreciable capacity for realistic analysis of world affairs phenomena—or at least that part of world affairs phenomena about which we queried them.

There remains to be discussed the actions taken by the people of Ridgeway to implement their attitudes on world affairs. Our conclusions are brief and our findings are negative regarding any such actions taken by the people of Ridgeway. We asked every person we interviewed what, if anything, he or she did to give effect to his conclusions about world affairs. We make the following observations.

---

[1] *Americans in World Affairs* (World Peace Foundation, 1959), pp. 2–3.

Voting

In the early part of the survey we asked each person what criteria were most important to him in choosing a president of the United States. We could not get answers, however, without suggesting them—and once we suggested a choice between the domestic and international policies of a candidate, the suggestion skewed the response. We were told most of the time that both criteria were important. More often we heard that the man rather than the party or the policy was the essential criterion. From the evidence gathered by the others and from our own impressions we lean toward the conclusion that domestic issues (particularly race and fiscal policy) are more vital than international issues. While we found many who like Senator Strom Thurmond, for example, we found none who could tell us (or apparently even cared) what the Senator's views on the United Nations are. Inside the town limits 92 per cent of the eligible Whites and 48 per cent of the eligible Negroes are registered voters. Most of the nonregistered Negroes intend to register. Of those we interviewed, the Negro vote inside the town limits totaled seven in 1960, twelve in 1964, and twenty-six intending to vote in 1968.

Letters

We found only one person—a leading citizen with important public responsibilities—who "occasionally" expresses his opinion on international affairs to his congressman. However, after ending our regular visits to Ridgeway, we were informed by another of the town's leading citizens that as a result of her discussions with us about the role of the individual in world affairs, she wired her Congressman to support the Food for Freedom program. She seemed very proud of her action.

Talk

Many persons reported that they talk about their views on international relations with other people in Ridgeway. Probably this is the single most important action the people take to give effect to their attitudes. This is a truism elsewhere as well.

Organizations and Contributions

We were unable to find anyone who is a member of any organization primarily concerned with world affairs. Nor did anyone report making any financial contributions to world affairs programs or projects except CARE and church mission work. One high school student had been active in a United Nations program one year. One lady reported having been involved in a UNICEF drive at one time. One elderly gentleman says that he has "never made a contribution to the U.N. because he has never been asked to contribute."

Generally and somewhat emphatically we conclude that Ridgeway—although certainly not the stereotype of a sleepy little Southern town—is not an activist community in the field of international relations.

While Hero concludes that only "very small minorities, somewhere around one per cent, depending on how high we set our standards, approach the upper poles of all four continua," we believe that the next generation of Ridgeway citizens is capable of meeting minimum qualifications of all four.[2] The same forces which are strengthening Ridgeway's abilities to meet her international responsibilities are very rapidly erasing all the significant regional differences which may previously have been characteristic of the Deep South's participation in the nation's international activities. Hero thinks the process will be gradual. The late Dean Charles Lerche believed that "everyone with an interest in world affairs will have to look South anxiously for many years."[3] We believe that what we have found in a close study of the small Deep Southern town of Ridgeway, South Carolina, shows it to be a part of the national mainstream. Unless the communications revolution of the past two or three decades can be repealed, the town of Ridgeway, South Carolina—and every other small town in America—will soon be nationalized beyond all but purely geographical recognition. Its children study the same textbooks, its postmen deliver the same magazines, its daily newspapers carry the same columnists and news services, its roads lead to the same "downtown," and above all its television news is broadcast by the same networks that serve the rest of the nation.

---

[2] Ibid., p. 105.
[3] *The Uncertain South: Its Changing Patterns of Politics in Foreign Policy* (Chicago: Quadrangle Press, 1964), p. 290.

A distinguished student of the South, our late colleague Dean Charles Lerche of American University, wrote in 1964 that "in its final rendezvous with America, the South will display and voice a complete range of international opinion. None of the attitudes it will incorporate, however, will any longer be especially Southern." [4] We have studied only one aspect of Southern opinion and in only one small town. But we have found ample evidence that the South is already well advanced toward its final rendezvous with America. It is a phenomenon of the 1960s—not of the seventies and eighties.

---

[4] Ibid., p. 288.

VI

METHODS USED TO COMPLETE THE STUDY

The Ridgeway Project was conducted under the joint auspices of the University of South Carolina Department of International Studies and San Francisco State College. Only two researchers were involved. Urban Whitaker is professor of international relations at San Francisco State College, on leave for the 1965–66 academic year as visiting professor of international studies at the University of South Carolina. Bruce Davis is a native of Lancaster, South Carolina, a graduate of Furman University, a former high-school teacher, and a graduate student in international studies at the University of South Carolina.

The primary target group was those persons residing within the town limits of Ridgeway. However, several other groups were also included and are described in Section A below. The primary method used was the personal interview. However, several other sources of information are described in Section B below.

A. Groups Studied

Four groups of people were identified, and each was divided, by race, into two subgroups. The four primary groups were:

Group I: All persons resident within the town limits.

Group II: All persons working within the town limits but residing outside.

Group III: All persons in the rural area outside town but served by the Ridgeway post office.

Group IV: All Winnsboro High School students resident either within Ridgeway (Group I) or in the rural area served by the Ridgeway post office (Group III).

[61]

Results were tabulated separately for each of the eight sub-groups and for each of the four primary groups. In addition, Groups I and II were then combined to form a total "daytime Ridgeway" category, and finally all of the groups were combined. The totals for each group are recorded in the table below:

	White	Negro	Total
Group I (residents)	237*	173	410*
Group II (workers)	20	24	44
Daytime Ridgeway	257*	197	454*
Group III		...	3058
(surrounding countryside)			
Group IV (students)	60	12	72

* These figures include a family of thirteen which has moved from Ridgeway since the project began. The correct figures for total residents and daytime Ridgeway as of April 1st, 1966, were 397 and 441 respectively.

No figures are available to give a racial distribution for the post office rural area. It is clear, however, that the proportion of Negroes to Whites is considerably higher in the out-of-town rural area than in the town itself. The figures for the four groups are not added together for several reasons. First, there would be duplications because the high-school students are also included in Groups I and III and because some of Group II are also in Group III. In addition, the postal rural routes serve some residents who live within the town limits.

The total number of formal interviews completed was 271. Of these 155 were in-town residents. With only nine exceptions at least one adult member of each of the 116 occupied houses in town was interviewed. Thirty-two of the 44 persons who live outside but work inside the town were interviewed.[1]

Excluding children under high-school (eighth-grade) age, personal interviews were recorded with more than 78 per cent of the residents within the town limits.

The fact that the respondents to our questionnaire did not remain anonymous has been noted by one interested observer of our research, who himself has a rich background of experience in social research of this kind, as possibly prohibiting an honest, candid re-

[1] This figure of 44 may be low because we did not make a systematic attempt to determine how many maids and other domestic employees were hired from outside the town limits.

sponse. We do not deny the existence of certain real advantages connected with anonymous replies. However, any advantage of anonymity is given up in the intensive interviewing of a small area. We think the fact that the respondent's identity did not remain unknown is cause for only minimal concern. This we believe because we are confident that we enjoyed the complete confidence of almost all those interviewed, that they understood our purpose for being there for what it actually was, and thought it worthy of their full, honest and polite cooperation.

It has also been suggested, by the same critic, that responses to ten specific questions by all interviewees would have yielded more credible findings. We reject this. Although all interviewees were asked the same basic questions, the most accurate appraisal possible of their attitudes entailed sometimes asking supplementary questions or rephrasing misunderstood basic questions. In short, different people require different questions. Consequently, we feel that flexibility in administering the questionnaire functioned as an indispensable safeguard against grossly inaccurate appraisals of attitudes.

B. Sources of Information

In addition to the interviews other sources of information utilized were: Books and articles about the area in general; local communications media including newspapers, radio and television; local meetings including school classes and church services; official records; and social gatherings.

1. BOOKS AND ARTICLES The bibliography of this report lists all the books and articles about the Deep South in general and South Carolina in particular that were studied as part of this project. Of these only *A Fairfield Sketchbook* by Julian Bolick specifically covers the town of Ridgeway. Detailed information about Ridgeway was also available in a fact sheet published by the State Development Board and a folder published by the Ridgeway Community Development Organization.

2. COMMUNICATIONS MEDIA All the newspapers, magazines, radio and television sources of information generally utilized in Ridgeway were monitored by the researchers. The only local public medium of communication, the weekly Winnsboro *News and Herald* was studied throughout the nine months' duration of the project (September 1965–May 1966).

3. LOCAL MEETINGS The following events were attended by both members of the research team: seventh-grade classes at Ridgeway Elementary School (integrated) and Geiger Elementary School (Negro); tenth-grade classes at Fairfield High School (Negro); eleventh-grade classes at Winnsboro High School (integrated); Sunday services at the Baptist, Presbyterian, and Episcopal churches (White); a monthly meeting of the Ridgeway Women's Club; and a community supper and games night.

4. OFFICIAL RECORDS Town and county officials made official records freely available for study of land ownership, voting results, and library utilization. Both researchers visited the county courthouse, Fairfield County Library, and the Ridgeway Branch Library.

5. SOCIAL GATHERINGS Both researchers were regularly invited to luncheons and dinners in the homes of Ridgeway's leading citizens and had many opportunities for long and leisurely conversations which were not formally recorded as interviews.

6. THE INTERVIEWS The primary source of information, however, was the interviews. These were of four types: (1) personal interview; (2) group interview; (3) mail questionnaires; and (4) informal conversations.

The only *formal group interview* was at Winnsboro High School, where seventy-two Ridgeway students participated. The questionnaires, asking for the same type of information acquired from their parents in individual personal interviews, were distributed and the students were asked to fill them out at their desks. However, it was not an altogether self-administered questionnaire. The students responded to each item on the questionnaire following an item by item explanation by the interviewer. (Appendix I is a copy of the form which was used.) Informal conversations—with information recorded later but not at the time of the interview—were held with many persons, including former residents, county school officials and teachers, county librarians, residents of nearby communities, and many others. These conversations provided some factual data and a great deal of helpful background information.

Personal interviews—with the date recorded at the time by the interviewer (Appendix I)—were, however, the primary source of information. While both interviewers were present at some of these meetings, the bulk of the work was done in private conversations with only one interviewer and one respondent present. Most of the information presented in this report was acquired in this way. Respondents were informed that the personal information (page one of Appendix I) would be kept entirely confidential and was to be used primarily for statistical correlations. The respondents were also asked whether they were willing to be quoted regarding their attitudes (page two of Appendix I) or preferred to have that information also guarded as confidential.

VII

RELIABILITY OF FINDINGS

The reliability of our findings varies a great deal from subject to subject. For example, we can claim close to 100 per cent reliability on our calculation of the size of Ridgeway's population as of April 1, 1966, but we are necessarily less certain of the figures indicating that only one person in Ridgeway is strongly opposed to the United Nations. We have commented on the reliability of the items as they were discussed in the body of the text. There are, however, a number of general reliability problems which bear on the results of the study and should be discussed in greater detail.

First, both interviewers are firmly convinced that wherever they have been willing to draw strong conclusions, the evidence is reasonably reliable. This is a primary advantage of the personal interview as a source of information. The reliability is heightened by other factors: we employed several cross-checking devices; we had several different kinds of contacts with most of the respondents; and we visited regularly in the community for nine months. We are quite convinced that the people of Ridgeway were generally as sincere and candid with us as they were friendly, cooperative, and genuinely interested in our research work.

Nevertheless we recognize a number of difficulties that tend to cast doubt on the validity of some of the results. Among these are: the fact that two interviewers were involved; the relatively long span covered by the interviews; deliberate attempts to mislead us; failures in communications between interviewer and respondent; and failure to interview every resident. Some comments on each of these items will be helpful.

[66]

Two Interviewers

Some distortions of the findings—particularly in regard to the classification of attitudes—is bound to result from the fact that there were two interviewers. From time to time we discovered that we were getting different answers partly because we were phrasing our questions differently. Some of the information we sought (for example, whether domestic or international criteria were more important to the respondent in selecting a presidential candidate) were invalidated because we were inconsistent in the way we asked the question. We were, however, aware of this general problem from the beginning of the project, and by frequent discussion of interviewing techniques we believe that we were able to avoid any serious skewing of results.

The Time Span Covered by the Interviews

There are at least two aspects to this problem. First, the world environment in which we asked our questions changed daily. Some interviews were conducted on days when the United Nations was headline news. For example, Pope Paul's highly publicized visit to the United Nations was in progress during one of our interviewing sessions. Other interviews, however, were in more quiescent periods when the weather or local politics dominated the news of the day. What we could not take account of were any changes in opinion that may have occurred during the nine months of interviewing. One well-informed critic of our research has noted that the period of interviewing—September 1965 through May 1966—was a placid period, making it impossible to measure the stability of public attitude during a time of public outrage. We do not share the view that this was a placid period. Evidence to the contrary is more than ample to mark this period as one of great social disturbance and upheaval. This was a period in which America's involvement in Viet Nam—an issue about which a sizable portion of Ridgeway's people are acutely cognizant and deeply divided—was becoming increasingly confused and questioned. At the United Nations the dispute over the obligation of member states under Article 19 of the Charter to pay their fair share of the cost of United Nations peace-keeping operations—an issue on which the United States considerably compromised, if not surrendered, its initially strong stand—was a prominent part of the day's top news. The fact that many respondents noted with displeasure the Soviet and French failure to submit to special peace-keeping assessments firmly indicated that they had a concerned awareness of this crucial issue. The period of interviewing also, as noted above, coincided with the papal visit to the United Nations. Furthermore this was a period in which the treasured tradition and prized practice of racial segregation—a tradition and practice which not a few in Ridgeway believe to have been decreed in heaven by God—was crumbling under the combined force of moral, economic, and legal pressures. Ridgeway's whites and Ridgeway's blacks were sharing for the first time the same public education facilities during this period.

The people of Ridgeway are deeply but calmly concerned with these issues. They have not been thrown into a state of shock and outrage by them. The fact that issues and events such as these have not been enough to send waves of shock and outrage through the people of Ridgeway leads us to believe that they are not really susceptible to the kind of excessive outrage which might cause capricious changes in public attitudes.

The second aspect of this problem is that after the first week or two nearly everyone in the community was aware not only of the fact that we were conducting a survey but in many cases of the specific questions we were going to ask. What we could not control was the amount of preparation done for the interview by the respondent. In at least one case (United Daughters of the Confederacy) and probably in others there was some group discussion of the United Nations undertaken to provide us with better-informed answers. In spite of one tip-off that "the leading citizens" decided early in the game what they would tell us, we do not believe that any serious damage was thus done to the project. In only one case was there evidence of a deliberate attempt to mislead us— and that involved only one minor question of personal information. Although one reviewer of our research suggested that the fact that the respondents were not getting paid for answers made their responses more valid, we feel that there was an obvious expectation of a psychic income, i.e., they were intrigued with the idea that the thinking of their town on world affairs in general and the United Nations in particular was going to receive national exposure; and they hoped to avoid any appearance of ignorance and unconcern. Not to appear ignorant and unconcerned on matters that should be of some concern to everyone is a universally normal human hope, and we believe the group discussion of the United

Nations by the United Daughters of the Confederacy and any preparatory discussions among the town's leading citizens were merely manifestations of that hope.

The possibility that the pro-U.N. flavor of our findings was the result of a deliberate attempt to tell us "what we wanted to hear" seems remote. While the people of Ridgeway might have assumed that we favored the United Nations (because we were associated with a university), they did not have hard evidence of this fact. We are strongly supported in this assumption by Alfred O. Hero, who has, in a long letter to the authors regarding our research findings, informed us that "the proportions who have in general approved of the U.N. and felt that we should remain members therein have been (at least since the end of the Korean War) large majorities in the South and only 3 to 5 percentage points below the non-Southern average. Even in racially troubled Bolivar County, Mississippi, and Wilcox County, Alabama, both with much larger percentages of Negroes than Ridgeway, no more than 10 per cent of our interviewees in the early 1960s expressed fundamentally hostile views on the U.N."[1] On other subjects it was clear that no attempt was made to display any artificial agreement with us.[2] Our own views on race relations and politics became better known than our views of the U.N., but the majority of the respondents expressed opinions different from ours on these issues.

Misunderstanding

In several cases—primarily with illiterates and near-illiterates—there is some evidence that the respondents gave definite answers to questions which they did not understand. Probably this was detected by the interviewer in most cases. Nevertheless it seems apparent that communications difficulties between interviewer and respondent introduced some degree of error. With respect to our most important questions (about the United Nations), we attempted to compensate for this problem by asking a number of extra questions designed to cross-check one answer with another and to determine whether the respondent knew what he was talking about.

---

[1] Letter, May 8, 1966, from Alfred O. Hero, managing editor of *International Organization* (Boston: World Peace Foundation).

[2] There was, however, one report that segregated classroom and lunchroom seating patterns were maintained in the integrated school except when it was known that a visitor was coming.

The Size of the Sample

We tried to interview every adult resident or employee in Ridgeway. We succeeded in talking with 78 per cent, including at least one adult in 92 per cent of the households. Although this "sample" is extremely large as public opinion polls go, it is still possible that some slight distortion is introduced in our results by the failure to include 22 per cent of the adults. But probably not. The 22 per cent were in the following categories: absentees (persons out of town for the year), the less available spouses of husbands or wives who were interviewed, the chronically ill or infirm, and those who simply refused to be interviewed (only one) or were never available (six households). The composition of the 22 per cent as a whole suggests that they were likely either to fit the usual pattern (especially spouses of those interviewed) or to be, in any case, among the less influential members of the community because they were usually absent or confined. However, there were a few interesting instances when spouses showed no hesitancy in taking opposing positions.

The most exciting exchange between husband and wife of differing opinions occurred between an elderly couple both of whom are college educated. The husband attended for three years, and his wife is a college graduate. They expressed notably different opinions at four points in the course of the interview. They registered their first difference when asked to indicate their 1960 presidential preference. The husband voted for Nixon, while his wife voted for Kennedy and "would vote for him again if he were living." Both voted for Goldwater in 1964. When asked which weighed heavier in their thinking when making a choice for president, the candidates' positions on domestic issues or international issues, the husband said domestic, noting that "we can't support and feed the whole world free of charge." His wife replied that both should be given equal consideration, noting that "when helping other people, you are looking out for your own people." While discussing their favorite political personalities, the husband expressed a strong liking for Strom Thurmond because "he stands up for his own opinions whether right or wrong." His wife, however, does not like Thurmond because "for one reason, he did such stupid things when elected governor, like standing on his head, etc." Their final disagreement unearthed by the interview concerned the prospects for U. S. involvement in another major war. The gentleman felt that "it will come sooner or later," while his lady felt "it could be avoided if the statesmen are of high enough calibre to see the way."

Where we have qualifications or doubts about the validity of conclusions, we have so indicated. But generally we believe that our most important findings are very reliable. We feel greatly buttressed in this belief by the fact that our findings do not serve as a self-fulfilling prophecy. In some important respects our research results did not square with our expectations. We began our study expecting to find that Southern Whites would feel generally negative about the United Nations—partly because of the U.N. human rights activities and partly as a by-product of general unilateralist sentiment. We expected to find significantly more opposition in the South as a region than in the nation as a whole. And we were fairly sure that the hard core of opposition to the U.N. would be found among rural Whites. Each of these assumptions proved to be false.

VIII

APPLICABILITY OF FINDINGS

Inevitably we have to face the question "So what?" For example, if Ridgeway gets most of its information on the U.N. from Huntley and Brinkley, does that mean that all of Fairfield County does, or that all of South Carolina does, or that the Deep South or the entire United States listens to NBC's news-reporting team by the whopping majority of 83 per cent?

We cannot claim that any of our findings will hold true for any group of Americans outside the town limits of Ridgeway, South Carolina. Yet it is likely that some of our results have more significant meaning than others. Some of them—for example, the firm evidence that television has more impact than radio or magazines as sources of world affairs information—may be valid for the United States as a whole. Some of the results, on the other hand, might not hold more than half a mile beyond the town limits.

The strong temptation is to apply all of the results to the Deep South as a meaningful unit. Except for occasional and cautious lapses we have by and large resisted this temptation. While we recognize that there are valid reasons for identifying "the South" or "the Southeast" as a region for some purposes, we believe that there are many "Souths." One of these may be the "Deep South," or Goldwater South, i. e., South Carolina, Georgia, Alabama, Mississippi, and Louisiana.[1] But even the five states of the "Deep South" are marked by enough significant differences to preclude

---

[1] In *The Deep South in Transition* (Tuscaloosa: Univ. of Alabama Press, 1964) Robert Highsaw, the editor, says, "It is accepted as a fact that there are many Souths" (p. 5). He and his colleagues define the Deep South to include these five states plus Florida.

their being thought of as a purely homogeneous grouping in all important respects. Perhaps this grouping represents the outer limit of valid generalization for any of our findings. In any case it seems necessary to consider the degree to which Ridgeway can be described as a "typical" small town in the rural Deep South. We make our consideration in three stages, looking first at the State of South Carolina, second at Fairfield County, and finally at the town of Ridgeway.

Is South Carolina a Typical Deep South State?

The Deep South is a geographically, culturally, politically, and economically distinctive region. Geographically South Carolina is the most northern (by only a few miles) and the most eastern of the five states. Still, all its borders (except the Atlantic) are with other Southern states, and it is clearly an integral part of the five-state band which forms (exempting Florida) the southeastern corner of the United States. In most other respects of Deep Southern distinctiveness South Carolina qualifies as typical. In some ways the state is more and in some ways less like the rest of the United States. For example, in the 1960 census only South Carolina and Mississippi (59 per cent and 63 per cent respectively) were more than 50 per cent rural.[2] South Carolina ranks at the bottom in average years of education and first among the fifty states in the number of selective service rejections for mental reasons. South Carolina was the first state to secede and remains very aware and very proud of its role in the Confederacy—yet it is clear that South Carolina's record of compliance with recent federal legislation places it in a decidedly different grouping from Mississippi, Alabama, and Louisiana. There have been no major civil rights disturbances in the State of South Carolina, and there are not likely to be any Selmas or Bogalusas.[3] However, South Carolina is not without its rabid racists who could have been stirred to equally nasty and despicable behavior at the time new civil rights laws were first being implemented and public schools and state universities were being integrated in response to federal directives.

---

[2] *The Deep South in Transition,* p. 8.

[3] Ernest M. Lander, Jr., *The Deep South in Transition,* p. 139, concludes that "there is no instance where a state in the Deep South voluntarily and freely granted any political right to the Negro race. Yet strangely, when forced to it, most Southern whites have accepted these changes in fairly good grace, in South Carolina and Georgia perhaps more than in Mississippi and Alabama."

But because of their relatively small number plus the fact that South Carolina is part of an older, more moderate, less brash tradition than Mississippi and Louisana, state and local leaders did not consider it politically imperative that they lead South Carolina's racial bigots in such demonstrations of defiance as occurred in Alabama, Mississippi, and Louisiana.

There are important differences and important similarities between South Carolina and the rest of the Deep South. Generally it must be concluded that South Carolina is properly included in the group of five Deep Southern states. Yet we do not argue that one would likely find the attitudes of Ridgeway's citizens to be typical of those in small towns of four hundred people in rural areas of Mississippi or Alabama. Probably there are similar towns in every state, but we have no evidence either to affirm or to deny the thought that Ridgeway is a typical Deep South rural town.

Is Fairfield County a Typical Rural South Carolina County?

With just over twenty thousand people in an area of 706 square miles (about the size of Rhode Island), Fairfield County ranks twenty-seventh in population among the forty-six counties of South Carolina. Only eight of the forty-six counties have a higher percentage of Negroes (59.5 per cent) than Fairfield. Only six counties have a higher percentage of functional illiterates (30.7 per cent) in the over-twenty-five age group. While Fairfield County ranks ninth in assessed valuation per pupil, it is thirty-second in expenditures per pupil, i. e., more money is available but less is spent on education. There is only one county in South Carolina (Clarendon, at 7.1 years) where the average adult school years is lower than in Fairfield County. In Fairfield the over-all average for adults is 7.3 years of education. For Fairfield Negroes the average is 5.4.[4]

Fairfield County, therefore, is not typical. Rather it is more rural, more sparsely populated, and—by a large margin—less educated than most of South Carolina. This is particularly significant in view of the fact that our findings reflect greater awareness and more liberal attitudes toward the United Nations than we would have expected. Some of this might be attributed to the fact that Fairfield County is adjacent to Richland County (including South Carolina's

---

[4] Figures provided by South Carolina Office of Adult Education and State Board of Education.

capital, its largest city, and the University of South Carolina).
Countering this factor, however, it is noted that Fairfield—with
only fifty students enrolled at the University of South Carolina—
is thirty-sixth among the forty-six counties in representation at the
university "next door."

Is Ridgeway a Typical South Carolina Rural Town?

We do not know. Our major concern is whether Ridgeway might
be a rare cultural oasis. If it is, then the applicability of our findings is severely restricted. Our evidence is not conclusive one way
or the other. We can only list those factors coming to our attention
which seem to point in one direction or the other.

By location Ridgeway has certain significant advantages not
accruing to all small towns. It is, for example, located at the highest point between Columbia (24 miles south) and Charlotte (72
miles north) and connected with both cities by good two-lane U. S.
highways. On the other hand, it is difficult to find any small town
in South Carolina which is not close to at least one major city.
Charleston, Savannah, Augusta, Greenville, Spartanburg, Charlotte,
and Florence form a circle roughly 100–130 miles in radius around
Columbia in the center of South Carolina. No South Carolina town
is more than an hour's drive from one of these cities. No South
Carolina town is more than about 130 miles from the capital city.

In education Ridgeway (11.5 years average) is clearly superior
to Fairfield County (7.3 years average). Yet we do not know how
this compares with the difference between other small towns and
their rural environs. Probably most small towns have higher educational averages than their environs, although there are some mill
towns or other factory towns composed primarily of working-class
residents, surrounded by a countryside of large homes of the managerial personnel and smaller residences of technical people. An
important part of Ridgeway's in-town population is composed of
managerial and/or semiretired personnel, while working groups
live mostly outside the town limits. But we have no comparative
figures for towns, and there is not much available for counties. We
do know that Ridgeway has a much higher proportion of Whites
to Negroes (60–40) than the Fairfield County total (40–60).
(Ridgeway and Winnsboro are the only two towns in the county.)

Politically it is hard to make a meaningful comparison between
Ridgeway and other small towns. We do know that Fairfield

County was typical of South Carolina in the 1960 presidential election (Kennedy, 1,633; Nixon, 1,549), while Ridgeway moved to the Republican column (Nixon, 129; Kennedy, 82). We know also that in 1964 Fairfield was atypical for South Carolina and more in line with the United States as a whole (Johnson, 2,628; Goldwater, 1,997), while Ridgeway was nearly 2 to 1 for Johnson (264–135). However, we have been unable to find a precise definition of "Ridgeway" for national electoral purposes. Clearly it includes a sizable part of the surrounding rural area. Very probably the strong Johnson vote was from the predominantly Negro suburbs. The only voting records which exist for the town of Ridgeway are those we compiled from our interviews. These indicate that Kennedy edged Nixon 44 to 36, while Goldwater trounced Johnson 57 to 33 inside the town limits.

Ridgeway has no high school, no newspaper, no medical doctor, no lawyer, and no full-time barber shop. It has four grocery stores within the town limits, a branch library, a bank and two elementary schools. It is just eleven miles by a major highway to Winnsboro, the county seat with about four thousand population. While we have made no study of this question, it seems apparent that Winnsboro is the first choice of Ridgeway citizens for services not available within the town. Columbia, less than half an hour away, is second. All Ridgeway high-school students are bussed to Winnsboro High School (integrated, but predominantly White) or to Fairfield High School (Negro) in Winnsboro.

Conclusions

We are frank to report that we cannot support with strong evidence any contention that Ridgeway is a typical Deep Southern rural area. Yet we are aware of no particularly strong evidence to the contrary. The people of Ridgeway themselves, while justly proud of their town, generally believe that they are not very different from most small towns in South Carolina.

Probably they are right. Probably it is not very different from most towns its size in the immediate surrounding countryside. Like most of them it has a long and proud history. Like all of them it is now under strong pressures from a host of technological changes. These two most vital influences—decades of conservative tradition and new forces for change—meet in almost every town of the five Deep Southern states. Beyond these all differences—and certainly there are notable differences even within a single state—are secondary in importance. Any generalization about the rural South which does not hold true in a town with Ridgeway's characteristics ought to be viewed with caution. Any generalization about Ridgeway which would be significant if it were true for the South as a whole ought to be given careful consideration.

Research into the attitudes of a whole region is an extremely difficult undertaking. Unless it involves hundreds of experts supported by hundreds of thousands of dollars, it cannot avoid one of two problems: an inadequately small sample for the large area covered, or an area too small to be clearly significant even with adequate coverage. Faced with a choice between these two dilemmas, we chose to do a thorough job in a very small area. We know that fewer than 1 per cent of South Carolinians live in towns of 200–500 population. (For South Carolina the exact figure is .86 per cent, for the Deep South as a whole it is .89 per cent.)[5] But we know that nearly 60 per cent of South Carolinians (compared with 49.5 per cent for the five states combined) are rural rather than urban residents. Most of them are near a town which they call "their" town. In the case of Ridgeway at least three thousand persons comprise the "community," although only about four hundred actually live within the town limits. While we concentrated primarily on the town itself, we interviewed a large sample of residents from the surrounding community, and we have expressed, above, considerable confidence in those results.

In conclusion we believe that our work should be viewed as a beginning effort. It stands in what we hope will be useful contrast to those research projects which have tried to study international attitudes in the South through small samples in widely scattered areas. Only if both kinds of studies are continued will we be able to learn more about the formulation of world affairs attitudes in the years of vastly increased international relationships which lie ahead.

---

[5] See complete population figures in Table F, p. 92.

APPENDIX I

1. H_____ _____   2. Address:_____Years_____

   W_____ _____   Previous: _____

   C_____ _____

3. Education: 1 2 3 4 5 6 7 8 9 10 11 12

   C1 C2 C3 C4   G1 G2 G3 G4

   Place: Major:

4. Income: approx. amt._____source_____Home: own rent

5. Church: Affiliation: Baptist Episcopal Presbyterian
   Methodist _____

   Attendance: strong regular weak nominal

6. Politics: Registration: yes no year_____

   Affiliation: D(lbj) I R(st) R( ) changed?

   Vote: 1960 Y N   1964 Y N

   Pres. choice: Nixon Kennedy Goldwater
   Johnson 1968_____

7. Community Position: Official Informal leader Normal
   Negligible

8. Organizations:

[78]

9. WORLD AFFAIRS INFORMATION SOURCES:

TV   yes   no   Channel_____

RADIO   yes   no   Station_____

NEWSPAPERS   yes   no   *State   Record   Winns* _____

MAGAZINES   yes   no

BOOKS   yes   no   library   own

TRAVEL   foreign: yes   no
          U. S.:   yes   no

LECTURES   often   occasional   never

OTHER

> (NOTE: This schedule was completed by the interviewers and
> was not shown to the respondent.)

10. FEELINGS ABOUT THE FUTURE

a. personal future: excellent   acceptable   not so good
     very poor   why?

b. U. S. in major war?   probable   possible   unlikely   no chance
     who?   when?   why?

c. General feeling about the world in 2000 A. D.
     strong optimism   tends to be optimistic   neutral
     tends to be pessimistic   strong pessimism

11. FEELINGS ABOUT THE UNITED NATIONS   first mention: int. resp.

a. never heard of it   heard of it but knows very little
     quite a bit of information   very well informed

b. specific source of U. N. info.

c. direction of feeling:
     strongly favorable   tends to be favorable   neutral
     tends to oppose   strongly opposes

d. reasons for feeling:

e. action to implement feelings:
     financial contribution   organization membership
     talk to friends   distribute literature   other_____

> May be quoted CONFIDENTIAL
> (NOTE: The interviewer marked one of these choices.)

APPENDIX II

CONFIDENTIAL (This information is for correlations only and will
not be shown to anyone.)

Name_____ Age_____ Address_____

EDUCATION (circle highest grade completed)
1 2 3 4 5 6 7 8 9 10 11 12
College 1 2 3 4   Graduate Work 1 2 3 4

CHURCH AFFILIATION: (circle one) Baptist, Presbyterian,
Episcopalian, Methodist   Other_____

POLITICS: Are you a registered voter? Yes_____ No_____

What is your party preference?_____

For whom did you vote in 1960?
Nixon_____ Kennedy_____

For whom did you vote in 1964?
Goldwater_____ Johnson_____

Who is your choice for President in 1968?_____

SOURCES OF INTERNATIONAL AFFAIRS INFORMATION:

Where do you get most of your information on world affairs:
If it is TV please specify the channel or the programs. If it is
magazines or newspapers please specify which ones. Feel free
to list several sources if that is the best description of your
situation.

Have you ever traveled outside the United States? Yes__ No__
If so, where and when?

Please go on to page two –

ATTITUDES

1. Attitudes About the Future in General

   a. Do you think your own personal future in the next 8 or 10 years will be:
   good?   bad?   why?

   b. Do you think the United States will be involved in another major world war?
   yes?   no?   when?   with whom?

   c. Do you think the school children of today will have a better world to live in than you have had so far?
   yes?   no?   why?

2. Attitudes About the United Nations

   a. How do you feel in general about the United Nations? Please circle one and make any comments you wish.
   strongly favorable   tend to be favorable   neutral
   tend to be opposed   strongly opposed
   Why?

   b. Do you think the United States should stay in the United Nations? Yes? No? Why or why not?

   c. Please feel free to make any other comments you would like about the U. N.

Please check one: _____ You may quote me. (from page 2 only)

                    _____ I wish to have all these comments remain confidential.

APPENDIX III—SUMMARY OF FINDINGS

Explanatory note: Four tables are presented below showing: 1) Basic data concerning the person interviewed during the Ridgeway Project (Table A); 2) Sources of World Affairs Information (Table B); 3) Attitudes toward the future (Table C); and 4) Attitudes toward the United Nations (Table D).

The findings are reported for four basic groups and several sub-groups as follows:

Group I		All residents of Ridgeway
Group IC	=	White residents
Group IA	=	Negro residents
Group II		All non-residents employed in Ridgeway
Group IIC	=	White employees
Group IIA	=	Negro employees
Group III		Suburban Ridgeway
Group IIIC	=	White suburban residents
Group IIIA	=	Negro suburban residents
Group IV		Ridgeway students of Winnsboro High School
Group IVC	=	White students 8-12th grade
Group IVA	=	Negro students 8-12th grade

Separate figures are given for each sub-group. Totals are given for each Group and a grand total (far right column) for all persons interviewed. In addition a sub-total is recorded for Groups I and II combined as "Daytime Ridgeway."

[82]

The number of persons interviewed varies considerably because some of the questions are not applicable to all respondents (for example, those under 21 are not included in voting tabulations, etc.). The maximum size of each group is as follows:

Group IC	105	
Group IA	35	
Group I		140
Group IIC	17	
Group IIA	14	
Group II		31
Group IIIC	10	
Group IIIA	18	
Group III		28
Group IVC	60	
Group IVA	12	
Group IV		72
GRAND TOTAL		271

Basic data was not collected in every case for high school students so only the first three groups are represented in Table A.

TABLE A—BASIC DATA ON RESPONDENTS

TYPE OF DATA	Group+Group=Group IC	IA	I	Group+Group=Group IIC	IIA	II	Groups I and II	Group+Group=Group IIIC	IIIA	III	Totals
AGE											
1. Average Age	47	42	46	48	45	47	46	51	42	45	45
2. Age Range	18-85	14-84	14-85	26-67	20-67	20-67	14-85	22-68	16-77	16-77	14-85
EDUCATION											
3. Average Years of Education	12.5	8.5	11.5	13.2	13.5	13.3	11.8	12.3	9.3	10.4	11.6
4. College Graduates	21.7	3.0	16.8	41.2	57.1	48.4	23.1	20.0	11.1	14.3	21.7
5. Some College	17.4	0	12.8	11.8	0	6.5	11.5	30.0	5.6	14.3	11.9
6. High School Graduates	31.5	21.2	28.8	23.5	14.3	19.4	26.9	30.0	16.7	21.4	26.0
RELIGION											
7. Baptist	55.8	60.0	56.9	43.8	64.3	53.3	56.2	40.0	88.2	70.4	58.1
8. Presbyterian	27.9	34.3	29.5	25.0	14.3	20.0	27.8	10.0	11.8	11.1	25.5
9. Episcopal	11.5	0	8.6	18.8	0	10.0	8.9	50.0	0	18.5	10.2
10. Others	4.8	5.7	5.0	12.5	21.4	16.7	7.1	0	0	0	6.1
POLITICS											
11. Democrats (National)	33.7	92.9	42.0	43.8	100.0	69.0	48.1	57.1	100.0	82.4	52.1
12. Democrats (States Rights)	7.0	0	6.0	0	0	0	4.7	0	0	0	4.1
13. Total	40.7	92.9	48.0	43.8	100.0	69.0	52.8	57.1	100.0	82.4	56.2
14. Independents	40.7	0	35.0	25.0	0	13.8	30.2	0	0	0	26.7
15. Republicans	18.6	7.1	17.0	31.2	0	17.3	17.1	42.9	0	17.6	17.1
16. Not Registered	8.0	52.0	18.0	0	7.0	3.3	15.1	0	33.0	22.7	16.1
VOTING											
1960 Kennedy	50.7	100.0	55.0	30.8	100.0	64.0	57.1	42.9	100.0	75.0	59.5
Nixon	49.3	0	45.0	69.2	0	36.0	42.9	57.1	0	25.0	40.4
1964 Johnson	26.9	100.0	36.7	16.7	100.0	58.3	41.2	0	100.0	66.7	44.1
Goldwater	73.1	0	63.3	83.3	0	41.7	58.8	100.0	0	33.3	55.8
1968 Johnson	14.9	92.3	35.0	7.7	80.0	39.1	35.8	14.3	100.0	66.7	39.7
Other Democrats	5.4	7.7	6.0	7.7	20.0	13.0	7.3	0	0	0	6.4
Nixon	14.9	0	11.0	46.2	0	26.1	13.8	0	0	0	12.1
Goldwater	6.8	0	5.0	7.7	0	4.3	4.9	28.6	0	11.1	5.7
Other Republicans	12.2	0	9.0	7.7	0	4.3	8.1	28.6	0	11.1	8.5
Anti LBJ	45.9	0	34.0	23.1	0	13.0	30.1	28.6	0	72.2	35.4

TABLE B—SOURCES OF WORLD AFFAIRS INFORMATION

TYPE OF DATA	Group IC + Group IA		= Group I	Group IIC + Group IIA		= Group II	Groups I and II
	%	%	%	%	%	%	%
TELEVISION							
1. Huntley-Brinkley	43.9	42.9	43.6	64.7	42.0	54.8	45.6
2. Other—Channel 10	44.8	37.1	42.9	17.6	50.0	32.3	40.9
3. Total NBC-TV	88.7	80.0	86.4	82.4	93.0	87.1	86.5
4. Other Channels	34.3	5.7	27.1	5.9	0	3.2	22.8
5. None	8.6	20.0	11.4	11.8	7.0	9.7	11.1
RADIO							
1. WIS	25.7	25.7	25.7	23.5	7.0	16.1	24.0
2. WCOS	2.9	0	2.1	0	0	0	1.7
3. WOIC	0	20.0	5.0	0	0	0	4.1
4. Winnsboro Stations	2.9	0	2.1	5.9	0	3.2	2.3
5. Others	21.9	14.3	20.0	11.8	14.0	12.9	18.7
6. None	50.5	45.7	49.3	58.8	79.0	67.7	52.6
NEWSPAPERS							
1. State	80.0	51.4	72.9	93.1	72.0	83.9	84.9
2. Record	23.8	11.4	20.7	23.5	14.0	19.4	20.5
3. Winnsboro News-Herald	25.7	0	19.3	5.9	0	3.2	16.4
4. Others	5.7	5.7	5.7	0	7.0	3.2	5.3
5. None	12.4	37.1	18.6	5.9	28.0	16.1	18.1
MAGAZINES							
1. Reader's Digest	15.2	0	11.4	17.6	14.0	16.1	12.3
2. Newsweek	9.5	0	7.1	5.9	14.0	9.7	8.6
3. Time	1.9	0	1.4	11.8	35.0	22.6	5.3
4. U. S. News and W. R.	8.6	0	6.4	0	0	0	5.3
5. Life	8.6	5.7	7.9	5.9	28.0	16.1	9.4
6. Look	11.4	8.6	10.7	0	21.0	9.7	10.5
7. Negro Publications	0	5.7	1.4	0	14.0	6.5	2.3
8. Others	49.5	14.3	40.7	40.2	58.0	48.4	42.1
9. None	38.1	74.3	47.1	58.8	28.0	45.2	46.8
TRAVEL							
1. Foreign	15.2	5.7	12.9	40.2	7.0	25.7	15.2
2. Domestic	30.5	25.7	29.3	47.1	35.0	41.9	31.6

TABLE B—SOURCES OF WORLD AFFAIRS INFORMATION—Continued

TYPE OF DATA	Group IIIC + Group IIIA = Group III			Group IVC + Group IVA = Group IV			Totals
	%	%	%	%	%	%	%
TELEVISION							
1. Huntley-Brinkley	77.0	50.0	59.3	20.0	25.0	20.8	40.4
2. Other—Channel 10	22.0	27.8	25.9	55.0	41.0	52.7	42.6
3. Total NBC-TV	100.0	77.8	85.2	75.0	67.0	73.6	83.0
4. Other Channels	11.0	5.6	7.4	1.6	0	1.4	15.5
5. None	22.0	11.1	14.8	1.6	8.0	1.4	8.9
RADIO							
1. WIS	11.0	11.1	11.1	6.6	8.0	6.9	18.1
2. WCOS	0	0	0	21.6	0	18.1	5.9
3. WOIC	0	5.6	3.7	0	8.0	1.4	3.3
4. Winnsboro Stations	0	0	0	6.6	16.0	8.3	3.7
5. Others	0	55.6	37.0	55.0	41.0	52.7	29.6
6. None	89.0	44.4	59.3	18.4	25.0	19.4	44.4
NEWSPAPERS							
1. State	55.0	55.6	55.6	68.3	41.0	63.9	70.0
2. Record	22.0	5.6	11.1	8.0	0	6.9	15.9
3. Winnsboro News-Herald	0	11.1	7.4	3.3	0	2.8	11.8
4. Others	22.0	5.6	11.1	14.9	16.0	15.3	8.5
5. None	33.0	44.4	40.7	13.3	41.0	18.1	20.4
MAGAZINES							
1. Reader's Digest	11.0	0	3.7	1.6	0	1.4	8.5
2. Newsweek	22.0	0	7.4	8.0	16.0	9.6	8.2
3. Time	11.0	0	3.7	3.3	0	2.8	4.4
4. U. S. News and W. R.	22.0	0	7.4	1.6	0	1.4	4.4
5. Life	0	22.2	14.8	20.0	16.0	19.4	12.6
6. Look	22.0	5.6	11.1	14.9	0	12.5	11.1
7. Negro Publications	0	11.1	7.4	0	0	0	2.2
8. Others	67.0	0	22.2	11.7	25.0	13.9	32.6
9. None	33.0	61.1	51.9	68.3	41.0	63.9	51.8
TRAVEL							
1. Foreign	44.0	11.1	22.2	5.0	0	4.2	12.9
2. Domestic	55.0	33.3	40.7	50.0	83.0	55.6	38.8

TABLE C—ATTITUDES TOWARD THE FUTURE

Column groups: Group IC + Group IA = Group I; Group IIC + Group IIA = Group II; Groups I & II. Reason rows are given as Opt. / Pess.; other rows are single %.

TYPE OF DATA	Group IC	Group IA	Group I	Group IIC	Group IIA	Group II	Groups I & II
PERSONAL FUTURE							
1. Optimism	54.2	31.4	48.1	47.1	100.0	71.0	52.5
2. Pessimism	27.1	11.4	22.9	35.3	0	19.4	22.2
3. No opinion	18.8	57.1	29.0	17.6	0	9.7	25.3
REASON *(Opt. / Pess.)*							
1. Race	0 / 7.3	0 / 2.9	0 / 6.1	0 / 5.9	7.1 / 0	6.5 / 3.2	1.2 / 5.6
2. Economic	15.6 / 7.3	8.6 / 5.7	13.7 / 6.9	23.5 / 11.8	21.4 / 0	22.6 / 6.5	15.4 / 6.8
3. Other	7.3 / 16.7	8.6 / 5.7	7.6 / 13.7	11.8 / 11.8	28.6 / 0	19.4 / 6.5	9.9 / 12.3
4. None	53.1	71.4	58.0	41.2	42.9	41.9	54.9
WAR							
1. Probable	25.0	11.4	21.4	17.6	21.4	19.4	19.9
2. Possible	38.5	20.0	33.6	35.3	21.4	29.0	31.3
3. Unlikely	19.8	8.6	16.8	29.4	21.4	25.8	21.3
4. No opinion	17.0	60.0	28.2	17.6	35.7	25.8	27.0
OPPONENT							
1. USSR	11.5	14.3	12.2	11.8	0	6.5	11.1
2. China	18.7	5.7	15.3	23.5	7.1	16.1	15.4
3. USSR or China	10.4	0	7.6	0	0	0	6.2
4. Other	13.5	8.6	12.2	17.6	14.0	16.1	13.0
5. Blank	45.8	71.4	52.6	47.1	78.6	61.3	54.3
ATTITUDES ABOUT 2000 A.D.							
1. Optimistic	28.1	42.9	32.0	35.3	92.9	61.3	37.7
2. Pessimistic	40.6	8.6	32.0	29.4	7.1	19.4	26.5
3. No Opinion	31.2	48.6	35.9	35.3	0	19.4	32.7
REASON *(Opt. / Pess.)*							
1. Economic	1.0 / 6.2	5.7 / 0	2.3 / 4.6	5.9 / 5.9	7.1 / 0	6.5 / 3.2	3.1 / 4.3
2. Moral	1.0 / 12.5	0 / 5.7	0.8 / 10.7	5.9 / 5.9	0 / 0	3.2 / 3.2	1.2 / 9.3
3. Political	0 / 1.0	0 / 0	0 / 0.8	0 / 5.9	0 / 0	0 / 3.2	0 / 1.2
4. Education	3.1 / 0	17.1 / 0	6.9 / 0	0 / 0	28.6 / 0	0 / 0	8.0 / 0
5. Race	0 / 5.2	8.6 / 0	2.3 / 3.8	0 / 5.9	0 / 0	3.2 / 3.2	2.5 / 3.7
6. Other	8.3 / 10.4	0 / 0	6.1 / 7.6	23.5 / 5.9	0 / 0	12.9 / 3.2	7.4 / 6.8
7. None	53.1	65.7	56.5	41.2	64.3	51.6	55.6

TABLE C—ATTITUDES TOWARD THE FUTURE—*Continued*

TYPE OF DATA	Group IIIC		+ Group IIIA		= Group III		Group IVC		+ Group IVA		= Group IV		Totals	
	%		%		%		%		%		%		%	
PERSONAL FUTURE														
1. Optimism	50.0		67.0		60.7		86.7		58.3		81.9		61.5	
2. Pessimism	30.0		5.6		14.0		3.3		8.3		4.2		16.4	
3. No Opinion	20.0		27.8		25.0		10.0		33.3		13.9		22.1	
	Opt.	Pess.	Opt.	Pess.	Opt.	Pess.	Opt.	Pess.	Opt.	Pess.	Opt.	Pess.	Opt.	Pess.
REASON														
1. Race	0	10.0	16.7	5.6	10.7	7.1	0	0	0	0	0	0	1.9	4.2
2. Economic	0	30.0	16.7	0	10.7	10.7	3.3	1.7	0	0	2.8	1.4	11.5	5.7
3. Other	20.0	10.0	16.7	0	17.9	3.6	35.0	1.7	25.0	0	29.2	1.4	15.6	8.4
4. None	40.0		61.1		53.6		58.3		75.0		61.2		56.5	
WAR														
1. Probable	60.0		11.1		28.6		25.0		25.0		25.0		26.8	
2. Possible	20.0		27.8		25.0		63.3		33.0		58.3		41.6	
3. Unlikely	10.0		22.2		17.9		11.7		8.3		11.1		14.5	
4. No Opinion	10.0		38.9		28.6		0		33.0		5.6		17.1	
OPPONENT														
1. USSR	30.0		5.6		14.0		20.0		8.3		18.1		13.4	
2. China	0		5.6		3.6		11.7		0		9.7		12.6	
3. USSR or China	10.0		0		3.6		3.3		0		2.8		5.0	
4. Other	0		5.6		3.6		10.0		0		8.3		10.7	
5. Blank	60.0		83.3		75.0		55.0		91.7		61.2		58.4	
High School Students Expecting to do Military Service							80.0		50.0		76.9		76.9	
ATTITUDES ABOUT 2000 A.D.														
1. Optimistic	30.0		77.8		60.7		53.3		33.0		50.0		43.5	
2. Pessimistic	50.0		5.6		21.4		15.0		17.0		15.3		22.9	
3. No Opinion	20.0		17.0		17.9		31.7		50.0		34.7		31.7	
	Opt.	Pess.	Opt.	Pess.	Opt.	Pess.	Opt.	Pess.	Opt.	Pess.	Opt.	Pess.	Opt.	Pess.
REASON														
1. Economic	10.0	20.0	5.6	0	7.1	7.1	0	0	0	0	0	0	2.7	3.4
2. Moral	0	0	0	5.6	0	3.6	0	0	0	0	0	0	.7	6.1
3. Political	0	0	0	0	0	0	0	0	0	0	0	0	0	.7
4. Education	20.0	0	11.1	0	14.0	0	0	0	0	0	0	0	6.5	0
5. Race	10.0	10.0	11.1	0	10.7	3.6	0	0	50.0	0	0	0	2.7	2.7
6. Other	20.0	10.0	11.1	0	14.0	3.6	1.7	3.3	0	0	1.4	2.8	6.5	5.3
7. None	30.0		61.1		50.0		95.0		0		95.8		66.0	

TABLE D—ATTITUDES TOWARD THE U. N.

TYPE OF DATA	Group IC + Group IA = Group I			Group IIC + Group IIA = Group II			Groups I and II
	%	%	%	%	%	%	%
Strongly Favor	32.3	11.4	25.2	23.5	35.7	29.0	27.2
Tend to Favor	27.1	25.7	26.7	52.9	35.7	45.2	30.2
Total Favorable	59.3	48.6	53.4	76.5	71.4	74.2	57.4
Strongly Oppose	1.04	0	0.8	0	0	0	.6
Tend to Oppose	9.4	0	6.9	5.9	0	3.2	6.2
Total Opposed	10.4	0	7.6	5.9	0	3.2	6.8
No Opinion	27.1	31.4	28.2	7.6	0	9.7	24.7
Neutral	0	0	0	0	0	0	0
Never Heard of It	3.1	31.4	10.7	0	28.6	12.9	11.1
REASONS							
Talk	17.7	2.9	13.7	35.3	14.0	25.8	16.1
Peace	21.9	2.9	16.8	47.1	21.4	35.5	20.4
Communism	0	0	0	0	0	0	0

TABLE D—ATTITUDES TOWARD THE U. N.—Continued

TYPE OF DATA	Group IIIC + Group IIIA = Group III			Group IVC + Group IVA = Group IV			Totals
	%	%	%	%	%	%	%
Strongly Favor	10.0	27.8	21.4	41.7	16.7	37.5	29.4
Tend to Favor	60.0	22.2	35.7	33.3	41.7	34.7	32.1
Total Favorable	70.0	50.0	57.1	75.0	58.4	72.2	61.5
Strongly Oppose	0	0	0	0	0	0	.4
Tend to Oppose	10.0	0	3.6	0	0	0	4.2
Total Opposed	10.0	0	3.6	0	0	0	4.6
No Opinion	10.0	17.0	14.0	23.3	33.3	25.0	23.7
Neutral	10.0	0	3.6	1.7	0	1.4	.7
Never Heard of It	0	33.0	21.4	0	8.3	1.4	9.5
REASONS							
Talk	10.0	22.2	17.9	6.7	8.3	6.9	13.7
Peace	30.0	0	10.7	15.0	0	12.5	17.2
Communism	10.0	0	3.6	0	0	0	.4

TABLE E—EXPECTATIONS OF CAROLINA AND CALIFORNIA STUDENTS

QUESTION: What attitudes toward the United Nations would you expect to find in a typical rural town of about 400 inhabitants in the Deep South? (The town in this case is Ridgeway, South Carolina.) Please indicate below what you think a social science research team would find in a study of this question.

1. The attitude toward the United Nations which would be characteristic of the majority of the *White population* would be:

	strongly favorable	tend to be favorable	neutral	tend to be opposed	strongly opposed
Carolina students	2.7%	60.8 %	6.5 %	26 %	4%
California students	3 %	36 %	13 %	42 %	6%
Actual Ridgeway attitudes	32.3%	27.1%	30.2%	10.4%	1%

2. The attitude toward the United Nations which would be characteristic of the majority of the *Negro population* would be:

	strongly favorable	tend to be favorable	neutral	tend to be opposed	strongly opposed
Carolina students	5.3%	21 %	69.8%	2.6%	1.3%
California students	4.7%	36.8%	42.4%	15.2%	.9%
Actual Ridgeway attitudes	11.4%	25.7%	62.8%	0	0

3. The percentage of the total population in favor of having the United States *continue* its membership in the United Nations would be about: 10% 20% 30% 40% 50% 60% 70% 80% 90% 100% (Nation-wide figure is usually 85–90% support of U.N.)

Carolina students	63.2%
California students	62.2%
Actual Ridgeway attitudes	over 90 %

(This figure of 90% excludes only those generally opposed to the U.N.—not those who were neutral or had no opinion.)

4. Support of the U.N. in Ridgeway would be:

	Carolina	California
Much less than in San Francisco	25 %	39.2%
Somewhat less than in San Francisco	47.4%	44.2%
About the same as in San Francisco	9.2%	9.8%
Somewhat more than in San Francisco	10.5%	5.8%
Much more than in San Francisco	7.9%	1 %

TABLE F—POPULATION STATISTICS

1960 U. S. CENSUS		S. CAROLINA	GEORGIA	ALABAMA	LOUISIANA	MISSISSIPPI	TOTAL OF 5 STATES
Towns 500–1,000	Number of Towns	37	90	69	41	59	296
	Population	24,740	61,906	50,834	29,728	40,106	207,314
	% of State Total Pop.	1.04	1.57	1.55	0.91	1.84	Mean: 1.38%
Towns 200–500	Number of Towns	62	154	76	55	63	410
	Population	20,389	49,814	24,544	18,704	22,185	137,836
	% of State Total Pop.	0.86	1.26	0.75	0.58	1.02	Mean: 0.89%
Towns Under 200	Number of Towns	36	124	35	11	30	236
	Population	5,175	14,593	4,798	1,550	3,970	30,086
	% of State Total Pop.	0.22	0.37	0.14	0.05	0.18	Mean: 0.19%
TOTAL POPULATION		2,382,027	3,943,116	3,266,740	3,257,022	2,178,141	16,030,146
Urban * Population:		981,386	2,180,236	1,791,721	2,060,606	820,805	7,834,854
	% of Total Population	41.2	55.3	54.8	63.6	37.7	Mean: 50.5%
	White Population	700,497–71.4%	1,533,418–55.3%	1,235,811–69%	1,415,592–68.7%	525,853–61.4%	4,960,196–63.3%
	Negro Population	279,935–28.5%	646,818–44.7%	554,619–31%	642,179–31.2%	293,672–35.8%	2,417,223–36.5%
Rural Population:		1,401,208	1,762,880	1,475,019	1,196,416	1,357,336	7,192,859
	% of Total Population	58.8	44.7	45.2	36.7	62.3	Mean: 49.5%
	White Population	850,525–60.7%	1,283,805–72.8%	1,047,798–71%	796,123–66.5%	731,693–53.9%	4,709,944–65.5%
	Negro Population	550,683–39.2%	479,075–27.1%	425,652–28.9%	397,028–33.2%	622,071–45.8%	2,474,509–34.2%

* Defined as > 2,500 Population.